Chilies to Chocolate

Chilies to Chocolate

FOOD THE AMERICAS GAVE THE WORLD

Edited by
Nelson Foster & Linda S. Cordell

The University of Arizona Press
Tucson & London

The University of Arizona Press
Copyright © 1992

The Arizona Board of Regents

♾ This book is printed on acid-free, archival-quality paper.
Manufactured in the United States of America

97 96 95 94 93 92   6 5 4 3 2 1

LIBRARY OF CONGRESS CATALOGING-IN-PUBLICATION DATA

Chilies to chocolate : food the Americas gave the world /
    edited by Nelson Foster and Linda S. Cordell.
      p.   cm.
    Includes bibliographical references and index.
    ISBN 0-8165-1301-5 (acid-free paper). —
    ISBN 0-8165-1324-4 (pbk. : acid-free paper)
      1. Food crops—America.   2. Food crops—Origin.
    I. Foster, Nelson.   II. Cordell, Linda S.
    SB176.A48C45   1992   92-5243
    641.3'097—dc20   CIP

British Cataloguing-in-Publication Data
A catalogue record for this book is available from the British
Library.

An earlier version of Jean Andrews's essay (Chapter 6) was
published in the *Journal of Gastronomy* 4:3 (Autumn 1988):21–35.
An earlier version of Noel Vietmeyer's essay (Chapter 7)
appeared in *Ceres* 17, no. 3 (May–June, 1984): 37–40.

Contents

v

CONTENTS

Preface

The origins of this book lie in a 1988 public symposium at the California Academy of Sciences. A book did not figure in plans for the symposium, but when the event sold out just days after it was announced and received an extraordinarily enthusiastic response from those in attendance, it became apparent that the topic of the symposium had a wider audience than expected and that a publication was in order.

The volume now in your hands is both less and more than the symposium's "proceedings." It can best be regarded as a collection inspired by the day's events. Several features of the symposium program, notably a magnificent festival of tastings put on by Bay Area restaurants, simply would not fit between book covers. (We trust readers to remedy this deficiency of their own accord.) Other parts of the program were set aside in favor of essays that better serve the needs of the anthology. It is these new contributions that make the book more than a proceedings report, bringing to it voices, subjects, and perspectives that were not heard in the academy's auditorium.

Both the event and the book were developed under the auspices of the academy's Department of Anthropology and with essential support from the Rietz Food Technology Foundation. We appreciate the trust placed in us by the members of the foundation's board—Betsy R. Dingwell, Sandra R. Jones, and Thomas Tilton.

Many colleagues and friends helped bring the two projects to fruition. Susanne Hirshen was responsible for organizing the symposium, and June Anderson and Tina Vincenzi handled most of its logistics. Several speakers enlivened the occasion with their knowledge and wit but are not represented in these pages: the eminent archaeologist Richard Stockton MacNeish, discoverer of the world's most primitive maize; Jerry DiVecchio, food and entertaining editor of *Sunset* magazine; well-known writer Raymond Sokolov, who specializes in food history and preparation; Nelly de Jordan, the "Betty Crocker of Bolivia" and a champion of native Andean crops; journalist and produce expert Sibella Kraus; and a trio of panelists—Narsai David, Mark Miller, and John Sedlar—who are renowned for their talent in preparing and discussing fine food.

We are grateful to the book's contributors not only for their essays but also for the perseverance and good cheer they demonstrated during the course of the book's preparation. Particular thanks are due to Gary Nabhan and Dan Early for counsel and collaboration beyond the call of duty or friendship. We are indebted as well to Stephen Cox, director of the University of Arizona Press, whose attention to the publication process has made our work a pleasure.

Introduction

NELSON FOSTER AND LINDA S. CORDELL

Some people have a very foolish way of not minding, or pretending not to mind, what they eat. For my part, I mind my belly very studiously, and very carefully; for I [judge] that he who does not mind his belly will hardly mind anything else.   Samuel Johnson

In an angry and admirable essay called "The Pleasures of Eating," Wendell Berry reminds "industrial eaters" (those of us who get our viands mainly by foraging at supermarkets and fast-food outlets) that eating "is inescapably an agricultural act, and that how we eat determines, to a considerable extent, the way the world is used." A farmer himself as well as a writer and social critic, Berry worries that, for many, "food is pretty much an abstract idea—something they do not know or imagine—until it appears on the grocery shelf or on the table." He implores us to build an acquaintance with our food by raising at least a little of it (in a pot or window box, if need be), by studying local sources, by trading directly with farmers whenever possible, and by learning the life histories of crops— their cycles of propagation, growth, flowering, fruiting, and decline.

This book offers another means of retrieving food from abstraction—to mind our bellies, as Dr. Johnson put it, and thereby to mind much more. It explores not the life history but rather the evolutionary and cultural trajectory of some of the great plants that feed us. Their stories read like biological and historical whodunits: Where did the wild ancestor of this plant arise? What people domesticated it? How and when? What did they do to adapt it? What part has it played in the life of their culture? When did other Americans and then Europeans get their hands on it? How did it spread to the ends of the earth—or why, despite its great merits, has it languished in obscurity? This book unravels some of these mysteries, and in doing so it heightens our pleasure in the food on the end of our forks. The sweetness of corn on the cob is sweeter for knowing the long, winding way by which it has come into one's hands.

Fully told, the stories of all the world's crops would begin roughly a hundred million years ago with the rise of flowering plants. For our purposes, however, the saga begins about eight thousand years ago, when hunter-gatherer peoples in both the eastern and western hemispheres independently arrived at agriculture as a new solution to the problem of obtaining food. Agriculture is now so integral to our culture that some may have difficulty conceiving of it as an invention, but that it was and, in reality, continues to be. We are still learning how best to plant, tend, reap, and adapt plants to increase the quantity, quality, and reliability of harvests and to minimize both the economic and environmental costs of cultivation.

Humankind has invested immense energy in agriculture, because upon it rests the whole of civilization. Without the abundance of the domesticated plants or the bounty of gardens, fields, and orchards, our forebears could not have established cities or states, and today's population would be unsupportable. It is crops that have made large, fixed settlements and great nations possible and that have furnished the wherewithal (and some of the impetus) for the advancement of writing, science, industry, and the arts. Hunter-gatherer cultures have been wise, rich, and good in their own right, make no mistake, but farming has been the sine qua non of the complex social form that we think of as civilization.

In the Western Hemisphere, the originators of agriculture —and civilization—were, of course, its indigenous peoples. By the time Europeans reached this land, all but a handful of Native American societies had made the transition to agriculture, using hunting and gathering mainly to supplement the produce of their fields. Some of these were irrigated fields, where agriculture was practiced intensively and in a highly productive fashion. A few animal species were domesticated in the Americas—llamas, both for wool and as pack animals; guinea pigs, turkeys, and at least one species of duck for meat—but in this hemisphere the prehistoric agricultural revolution centered on plants.

Native gatherers, farmers, and crop breeders identified and developed the potential latent in the American flora, handing down to us a wealth of nutritious and pleasing plant foods. From the American cornucopia poured wild produce such as blueberries, cranberries, black walnuts, and wild rice; many kinds of produce from plants that were tended but not domesticated, including vanilla beans, cactus fruit, and Jerusalem artichokes; and numerous domesticated crops—maize, beans, pumpkin and squash, potatoes, and tomatoes, among others.

Crops of American origin constitute an impressive array of vegetables, grains, root crops, nuts, fruits, and spices. Rather than attempting an encyclopedic treatment, this book explores a few of the American crops, concentrating on species that have worldwide economic importance already or that might someday achieve it. Even after applying this principle of selection, we have had to exclude many valuable crops familiar to North Americans—peanuts, pecans, cashews, pineapple, papaya, avocado, sunflowers, sweet potatoes, and allspice, to name a few. (For a more extensive listing of American food plants, please consult the Appendix.)

All these crops were unsuspected by even the greatest minds of Asia, Africa, and Europe until five hundred years ago, when Cristobal Colombo, today better known as Christopher Columbus, blundered into the Caribbean. At the time, Europeans were still taking the measure of their own hemisphere. Only two centuries earlier, Marco Polo had returned to Venice from an overland trip, reporting the unbelievable affairs of an immense empire called China. Just a few years before Columbus's crossing, Portuguese navigators had rounded the southern tip of Africa and ventured for the first time into the Indian Ocean. The existence of another great landmass beyond Asia was so unimaginable that Columbus always believed he had reached Asia.

The peoples, plants, animals, landscapes, languages, and traditions of the American hemisphere were strange enough to the Europeans that, once they reconciled themselves to the fact that it was *not* Asia, they regarded the place as literally a New World. French archaeologist François Bordes suggests the extent of the surprise in his observation that a shock of equal magnitude is unlikely to occur unless intelligent life is found elsewhere in the universe. The encounter upset both European and American conceptions of earthly order and celestial intentions, and its consequences, for better or for worse, irrevocably changed the lives of the peoples of both worlds. The short-term impact on the Americas was little short of disastrous—enslavement, epidemics, and famine for its peoples and devastation of its lands, economic infrastructure, and cultural monuments.

Arguably the best part of the exchange was the Europeans' acquisition of American crops. Native Americans had begun with a very different wild flora than had the peoples of the Old World, and they had followed different tastes, interests, and procedures in developing their crops. Thus, few of the plants cultivated in the Americas were recognizable to Columbus, but having come for spices and being desperate for anything that might recover the cost of his voyage, he carried back to Europe a sizable assortment of seeds and live plant specimens. Later explorers, conquistadors, and colonists followed suit, and by the early sixteenth century, American crops had commenced a helter-skelter progress around the globe that continues even today.

As Alan Davidson makes plain in the first chapter, the Old World's reception of New World crops was far from regular or predictable. Some struck the European fancy and were soon successfully transplanted into royal hothouses and experimental gardens, incorporated into existing cuisines, and appreciated as worthy additions to the food supply and to the panoply of flavors. These were exceptional cases, however, because until modern times, societies usually absorbed new foods slowly, clinging instead to those that were familiar, those central to their cultures. For this reason, equally fine American crops were rejected or went unappreciated until their virtues were later discovered, often as a result of economic necessity. Through quirks of history, some worthy crops never found niches except in remote corners of the Old World and still have not found their way into its agricultural and culinary mainstreams.

However erratic and inexplicable the process, in the ensuing centuries New World crops radically transformed Old World eating. That juicy American berry the tomato brought new life to Italian food. Potatoes came to dominate the fields of Ireland, first to the delight of its people, later to their sorrow. They also occupied a prominent place on the tables of

England, France, and northern Italy. Koreans, Chinese, East Indians, and Hungarians welcomed hot chili peppers into the very heart of their national cuisines. Corn found favor widely and in many forms—eaten straight off the ear, ground for mush, baked into breads, even miniaturized to suit Chinese tastes. Peanuts took root in Southeast Asian cuisine, emerging in Thai and Vietnamese dishes and blending with chili peppers to yield the illustrious Indonesian *gado-gado* sauce. The bitter cacao bean won devotees around the world in its refined form, as chocolate.

This brief recital of the culinary consequences of 1492 conveys a sense of the tremendous influence that New World crops have had and illustrates the reality of the interdependence of cultures long before that subject became fashionable. But the Old World's appropriation of American crops has produced effects of greater magnitude and seriousness. Throughout the hemisphere, land too poor in soil, too high, too dry, too wet, too cold, or too hilly to support the Old World cereal grains of wheat, rice, barley, and rye has been successfully planted in the American staples of potatoes, maize, sweet potatoes, and manioc. Potatoes and maize now rank with wheat and rice as the world's four principal crops, while sweet potatoes and manioc (also known as cassava) serve as dietary mainstays for peoples of many nations, especially in the wet tropics and subtropics of Africa, Asia, and the South Pacific.

Thus crops of American origin sustain a large proportion of the Earth's present population. Old World staples—wheat, barley, rice, soybeans, and so forth—have come to the New World, too, contributing substantially to the food supply. But as Alfred Crosby concludes in his landmark book *The Columbian Exchange*, the fact that American crops thrived in adverse conditions gave them a critical role in the world population boom of the past two centuries; such a boom probably could not have occurred without them. Further growth in the human population might still be supported if the obscure New World plants discussed in this book—quinoa, amaranth, and Andean root crops such as ulluco—were more broadly established.

As this last point implies, the stories our authors tell are all unfinished. Much remains to be discovered about the genetic and cultural history of even the most important, most thoroughly studied American crops, and the future of each hangs on research, debate, decisions, and actions that lie ahead. We hope that this book, besides increasing the pleasure of eating, will engage its readers with the questions yet to be answered, especially those that require our responses as informed buyers, eaters, users of land and water, parents, workers, entrepreneurs, stockholders, and voters.

Consider the prospect raised above: the continued improvement and dissemination of American crops as a means of sustaining population growth. Until recently, challenging the importance or ethical basis of such an endeavor would have been unthinkable; it always seemed apparent that greater harvests were necessary and good. But in view of the toll already taken on the planetary ecosystem by rising numbers of *Homo sapiens* and by the intensified cultivation of land ("marginal" or otherwise), surely this is a subject that demands broad public consideration. Loss of topsoil, global climate change, reduction of the ozone layer, destruction of tropical rainforests, decline of biological diversity, dwindling of water resources and of petrochemicals used in fertilizer, accumulation of pesticides and herbicides in soil and in animal tissues—all these factors suggest that the time has arrived to renounce civilization's age-old project of wresting ever more benefits from Earth's finite means.

This and other issues of public policy surface throughout

the book, and several are treated in more depth in Gary Nabhan's epilogue. No effort was made to unify our contributors' views on these matters, but we are pleased to note one theme that runs strongly throughout the volume: the debt that all of us owe to Native American farmers and the responsibility this creates to ensure their descendants lasting and meaningful opportunities to grow, cook, consume, celebrate, develop, and exchange traditional crops. The fact that indigenous agricultural communities serve as gene banks for mainstream agriculture adds an urgent pragmatic reason for preserving Native Americans' options to live and farm in keeping with their traditional ways. Dislodging native farmers from their lands, water sources, and cultural foundations must end.

Consensus on this question does not imply agreement on others. When it comes to mainstream agriculture, the book's contributors fan out across a continuum between deep faith in its virtue and enduring promise and profound concern about its long-term social and environmental costs. Whatever place one occupies on this continuum, there can be no doubt that our society is wedded to large-scale agriculture. The issues of the day must be evaluated in that context and, we would add, with a keen appreciation for the sweat, sacrifice, ingenuity, and perseverance that has made modern farming and agricultural research so magnificently productive. Beyond expanding the sheer amount of food available, modern agronomy has brought new crops into being, increased the usefulness of many others, and vastly expanded our knowledge of plants.

Its very success has given the food industry the weight and momentum to roll over small farmers, native or otherwise. Though this sometimes occurs unintentionally and, in the long run, will surely work to the detriment of modern agriculture, it has been a pronounced trend in recent decades. The lessons of agricultural ecology are bringing increased respect for the sagacity of small farmers and their importance to the agricultural enterprise as a whole, but the tendency to monopolize agricultural resources for mainstream use still prevails. Thus we join Wendell Barry, Gary Nabhan, and others in calling for vigilance on the frontier where small-scale farming encounters its giant relation.

Minding our bellies is not a simple task and probably never has been. It requires not only sensitive taste buds and the willpower to refuse third helpings but also a broad understanding of the food on our plates. For early humans it required close and sustained attention to the shift of seasons and the places where fruits, nuts, greens, and seeds were available. For us today, if we would rather be diners in the global village than "industrial eaters," it requires attention to information and perspectives from diverse disciplines—archaeology, anthropology, history, botany, agronomy, genetics, gastronomy, and the crossover discipline of ethnobotany. All of these disciplines are brought to bear in the chapters that follow. Experts in any one field may regret the eclecticism of this approach, but we hope that lay readers, for whom this anthology is designed, will find it richly rewarding.

Chilies to Chocolate

CHAPTER I

Europeans' Wary Encounter with Tomatoes, Potatoes, and Other New World Foods

ALAN DAVIDSON

I wonder how Christopher Columbus felt as he sailed back eastward across the Atlantic. Triumphant? After all, he thought he had done what he set out to do: reach India. Or did he feel a little apprehensive? Did he have enough to show for the expense of the voyage—in particular, enough spices? Some of his specimens were rotting and had to be thrown overboard. How many would be viable, even just for study purposes, by the time he got back to Spain?

I imagine that he felt quite anxious, and I am sure that, though he was a man of vision, he had no conception of the magnitude of the exchange between the Old World and the New—of plants, animals, and diseases too—that his voyages would inaugurate. Rocking about in his tiny bark, throwing rotten plants over the side, his thoughts must have been on the immediate future.

We, of course, look at all this through the other end of the telescope. Even now, we do not know the end of the story, which will go on unfolding indefinitely, but we are privileged

I

to live at a time when we can survey its first five centuries, a period that has produced the greatest change in historical times. One strand of the story concerns what happened on the receiving end, how the American foods were received in Europe.

Though foods of American origin have had a worldwide impact, of necessity I shall limit my comments to Europe, and out of the scores of important foods America has given the world, I shall discuss in detail just two: the tomato and the potato. Both have particularly interesting histories, and both belong to the botanical family Solanaceae. We shall see how this relationship affected attitudes toward them when they arrived in Europe. I shall not, by the way, take up space discussing exactly when and how these plants arrived in the various countries of Europe and elsewhere in the Old World. These are interesting questions, to be sure, but my theme is what happened after their arrival—or what did not happen.

A few further comments by way of preamble. For obvious reasons, most of the new foods arrived first in Spain, the starting and finishing point of Columbus's voyages. Even allowing for the fact that botany was already being conducted on an international basis, with specimens freely exchanged, we must expect that Spanish attitudes and views about food would have played a major role in determining the reception of the new foods. In this connection it is appropriate to recall, first, that Spain lies in the southwest corner of Europe, facing southward across the Mediterranean, almost adjacent to North Africa, and, second, that it has had close historical links with the Arab world and has been much influenced by Arab cookery. Note, too, that in Columbus's day Seville, on the Mediterranean coast, was by far the most important port for receiving, and to some extent also disseminating, foodstuffs and other materials from the New World.

Finally, let us remember that from our vantage point in the twentieth century it seems self-evident that the foods we are discussing are indeed foods, but the Spaniards who encountered them in the period following Columbus's voyage of 1492 may well have perceived them very differently. Whether or not they knew that such things were being eaten by the American natives, the Spaniards' own feelings about them would have been determined to a large extent by their ability to fit them into the European scheme of things, to make analogies between them and familiar European foodstuffs, to detect potential commercial value, to spot potential difficulties in processing, and so on.

The beans of the New World, for example, were recognized as obviously akin to the beans of the Old World and likely to be similarly useful. Naturally enough, the New World beans were quickly brought into use in Europe. Although there is a tantalizing lack of precise information about how they spread, there are plenty of indications that they were being widely grown in Europe in the sixteenth century.

Likewise, maize was a bread-making cereal grain, something long familiar to Europeans. Given the fundamental importance of cereals, it is not surprising that maize, too, traveled fast and was soon the subject of experimentation, initially in the Middle East, which accounts for its later being called "Turkie wheat" and similar names in Europe. It was also accepted very quickly in Africa, where it proved to be a more prolific crop than sorghum, and later in the Balkans, where it thrives especially well and has become, for example, the staple food of Romania.

Chocolate was a different matter. An analogy was eventually made with coffee, and chocolate then could be slotted into place as a luxury beverage with stimulating qualities, calling for a ceremonial kind of service and fetching a high price. But it had no immediate slot in the Spanish conception of food and had to wait until the seventeenth century before it began its European career. Another such beverage, *maté*, had to wait even longer; indeed, it has still not really arrived.

The pineapple had to wait as well, for it was unlike any European fruit. It was treated first as a botanical curiosity and then as a challenge to gardeners with hothouses: could they induce it to fruit in Europe? A famous painting, made by Henry Dankerts in 1670, depicts Charles II receiving the first pineapple to be grown in England, but it was not until 1732, when Richard Bradley published the second of his two cookery books, that a recipe for the novel fruit appeared in English.

Spices were extremely important in medieval cookery and as an article of international commerce; anything in the nature of a new spice was likely to be seized on at once. So the chili pepper, as the source of a new, hot-tasting spice, was immediately whisked across the Atlantic to Spain—and on to the Near East, Asia, and East Africa. Medieval Europe also made much use of color in foods. The utility of annatto in producing a red color was quickly recognized, and it was not long before it, too, was adopted in Spain and elsewhere.

On the other hand, tropical root vegetables that require special treatment to be rendered safe and edible had no immediate attraction to the Spaniards or anyone else in Europe. They were unfamiliar, difficult to process, and potentially dangerous. Thus manioc (cassava), today a principal food resource in tropical regions worldwide, got off to a slow start.

Now we come to a different category, that including the potato and tomato and also the peanut. These must have been baffling to the Spaniards. The potato was the first vegetable of their acquaintance to be grown from tubers rather than from seed. Its appearance seemed as odd as its method of propagation, and under the prevailing Doctrine of Signatures, whereby a fruit or vegetable's appearance indicated what part of the body it would affect (hence walnuts being recommended for diseases of the brain and red beets for anemia), it was even thought that eating potatoes led to leprosy, for the tubers or flesh-colored underground nodules were likened to leprous growths. Moreover, the plant itself had a slightly sinister appearance, bearing a resemblance to deadly nightshade, a fellow member of the family Solanaceae. This led people to believe that the potato was poisonous, a belief that John Ruskin upheld even in the nineteenth century. On top of all this, it must have become known that the potatoes themselves were subject to strange treatments in South America, such as the freezing and dehydration and leaching that occur in the preparation of *chuño* and *tunta*, two forms of dried potato.

The purpose of the tomato would have posed a somewhat different question. Indeed, its purpose was not at all clear. It resembled a fruit, but it was acidic, too much so to be used as a fruit. Yet it was also unlike any familiar vegetable. "What is it?" the Spaniards must have asked themselves. As for the peanut, it seemed to be a nut, but whoever heard of an underground nut? Understandably, these foods did not at once grip the imagination and appetite of America's invaders.

Given this background, let me now treat two of the foods in more detail. The tomato may be best introduced with a passage from Flora Thompson's well-known trilogy *Lark Rise to Candleford*, which records its first arrival in the English hamlet of Lark Rise:

> It was on Jerry's cart tomatoes first appeared in the
> hamlet. They had not long been introduced into this
> country and were slowly making their way into favour.

The fruit was flatter in shape then than now and deeply grooved and indented from the stem, giving it an almost starlike appearance. There were bright yellow ones, too; as well as the scarlet; but, after a few years the yellow ones disappeared from the market and the red ones became rounder and smoother, as we see them now.

At first sight, the basket of red and yellow fruit attracted Laura's colour-loving eye. "What are those?" she asked old Jerry.

"Love-apples, me dear. Love-apples, they be; though some hignorant folks be a callin' 'em tommytoes. But you don't want any o' they—nasty sour things, they be, as only gentry can eat. You have a nice sweet orange wi' your penny." But Laura felt she must taste the love-apples and insisted upon having one.

Such daring created quite a sensation among the onlookers. "Don't 'ee go tryin' to eat it, now," one woman urged. "It'll only make 'ee sick. I know because I had one of the nasty horrid things at our Minnie's." And nasty, horrid things tomatoes remained in the popular estimation for years; though most people today would prefer them as they were then, with the real tomato flavour pronounced, to the watery insipidity of our larger, smoother tomato.

This happened in the last decade of the nineteenth century, just a hundred years ago. Reading it the other day brought home to me, with a vividness that history books rarely achieve, just how recent the popularity of the tomato in England is.

The first tomatoes to appear in Europe were, so far as we can tell, red ones. However, the name that was applied to them, with variations, in a number of languages was *pomodoro* (the Italian version) or *pomme d'amour* (the French), meaning respectively golden fruit and love fruit. Yellow and even whitish varieties of tomato existed in America, but this fruit was not golden and had no reputation as an aphrodisiac.

Dr. Rudolf Grewe, in an admirable paper that he delivered at a symposium in Konya, Turkey, in 1986, has solved this little mystery. He points out that the tomato is a close relative of the eggplant and was at first taken to be a kind of eggplant. The eggplant was called *pomme des Mours*, fruit of the Moors, because it was a favorite vegetable of the Arabs, and this was mispronounced as *pomme d'amour*. A similar process made it *pomodoro* in Italy, which it still is.

All this explains perfectly why the tomato, when it first appeared in European books in the 1550s, was given the Italian name *pomi d'oro*. The illustrations of the tomato in these early books—for example, in later editions of Dodoens's *Cruydy-Boeck*, first published in Antwerp in 1554—show the fruit with rather a flat top and bottom and numerous lobes or indentations (very different from the conventional round, smooth tomato of the present day), and repeated reference is made to the fruit's acidic taste.

It was not until 1590, when José de Acosta's *Historia natural y moral de las Indias* was published in Seville that Spanish readers received an indication that the tomato could be used in sauces. Acosta's observation was based simply on Indian usage. A couple of years later, a little book by Gregorio de los Ríos, a priest-gardener who worked in the botanical gardens at Aranjuez near Madrid, described tomatoes, adding: "It is said that they are good for sauces." This comment does not sound as if it were based on personal experience, and none of the Spanish cookbooks of this period mention the tomato.

The situation began to change in the next century. Grewe reports: "There is a painting in the Louvre that has haunted me since I first saw it years ago. Painted by Bartolomé Murillo in 1646 for the Franciscan convent of Seville, it is popularly entitled 'The Angels' Kitchen.' The right side of the painting shows angels preparing a meal. In an inconspicuous corner, we see a tomato, two eggplants, and a kind of pumpkin. Obviously in Seville, by 1646, the tomato had become a familiar and easily recognized culinary object."

This pictorial evidence is convincing, but it is nonetheless true that we do not find recipes for tomatoes until 1692 to 1694, which years saw the publication of *Lo scalco alla moderna* by the Italian writer Antonio Latini. His handful of tomato recipes include the first published recipe for tomato sauce and were all labeled "*alla Spagnuola*"—that is, in the Spanish fashion. The book was published in Naples, which was then part of the Spanish empire. This of course reminds us that the European countries had not yet taken on their modern form, and it can be misleading to speak of Spain and Italy and the Netherlands as though they were then the modern countries bearing these names. With this proviso, I return to Italy.

A professor who has made a particular study of Italian food of the seventeenth and eighteenth centuries tells me that until the latter part of the eighteenth century, tomatoes were luxuries for the well-to-do. Then gradually they came to be eaten by all classes, a change that took full effect in the nineteenth century and coincided, she thought, with the spread of pizza.

Earlier there had been several obstacles to its acceptance. One was suspicion of the strange new fruit. Another was its acidic taste, which was very pronounced in early times. A third was that no way had yet been found of keeping it. This was very important because what poorer Italians needed above all were foods that would keep. People could and did cook tomatoes and keep them in jars for a while, but it was not until a worthy man named Cirio thought of canning them that their cultivation on a large scale, not just for local consumption, became possible.

Meanwhile, in England the tomato was progressing just as slowly. Hannah Glasse, author of the most famous English cookbook of the eighteenth century, *The Art of Cookery Made Plain and Easy* (1747), refers once or twice to "love-apples," but it is clear that the tomato was still little known in the early part of the nineteenth century and that, so far as people in rural districts were concerned, it did not enter the kitchen until the end of the century. Witness the quotation from *Lark Rise to Candleford* with which I began this discussion.

In summary, the tomato was conspicuously slow to be adopted in Europe, and in this connection it is interesting to compare the fortunes of one of its relatives that came to Europe from the east rather than the west. I refer to the aubergine, or eggplant, which was of Asian origin, a great favorite among the Arabs but still very much a novelty for Europeans in the sixteenth century. Elizabeth David once wrote an essay about the eggplant entitled "Mad, Bad, Despised and Dangerous"—all epithets that she had found applied to it in herbals and other works of sixteenth-century Europe, especially those of Italy. Castor Durante, whose *Herbario Novo* came out in 1585, conceded that it was eaten (boiled like mushrooms or pickled) but gave a long and discouraging list of illnesses it could cause or worsen. In the following century, Antonio Frugoli described eggplant as a low-class food eaten by the Jews. This odd piece of information or prejudice, of which I have seen no explanation, was echoed with respect to tomatoes by the famous food writer Pellegrino Artusi, who asserted in 1880 that "forty years ago they [tomatoes] were scarcely to be seen in the Florence market, being regarded as base Jewish food."

In France there is little evidence of eggplant being used in the two or three centuries following its arrival. Even toward the end of the eighteenth century, a dictionary asserted that its only use was in making poultices for certain medical purposes. Not until the first part of the nineteenth century, when eggplant was promoted by Decoufle, a Parisian specialist in early vegetables, did it begin to appear as a foodstuff and to figure in recipes.

In Spain, however, the picture was different. Near the beginning of the sixteenth century, Ruperto de Nola gave four recipes for the eggplant in a cookery book that appeared first in Catalan and then in Spanish. Jumping ahead, we find eggplant as prominent as any other vegetable in Juan de Altamiras's little cookbook of 1817. The explanation for this early acceptance in Spain is, presumably, the Arab influence on its cuisine.

What we learn from this little digression is that generally speaking the eggplant had as hard a battle to win acceptance as did the tomato. We may infer from this that there was nothing about New World fruits that made them intrinsically more liable to receive a suspicious reception than those arriving from the more familiar source of Asia.

Of the foodstuffs that moved from the New World to the Old, maize has perhaps proved to be the most important, but the potato, I think, takes second place. Certainly it does if one is thinking of Europe. There are grounds for arguing that the great population increase on that continent in the eighteenth and nineteenth centuries was due, to a significant extent, to the adoption of the potato as a food.

Yet the potato was slow to cross the Atlantic. The Spaniard Nicolás Monardes does not mention it at all in his popular book on animals and plants introduced from the New World, which was published in successive editions during the 1560s and 1570s. In fact, the potato had to wait about a hundred years before it was first referred to in print. Then, at the end of the sixteenth century, it suddenly started to appear—in John Gerard's *Herbal* of 1597, for example.

The explanation seems to be that the conquistadors saw the potato being used as a food by the Native Americans, fed it to slaves, and even began to eat it themselves but failed to see in it anything that would be of use in Europe. This may seem to us, with the benefit of hindsight, to have been an extraordinary failure, but the conquerors were, after all, faced with a bewildering number of strange plants and foods, and it is not altogether surprising that they missed the potential significance of some, especially those whose habits of growth were mysterious. I have already alluded to some of the reasons why the potato was viewed with suspicion.

Despite such doubts, the potato was being grown in Spain by the 1670s. This information, culled from the account books of a hospital at Seville, is among the wealth of material gathered together by the late Redcliffe Salaman in his massive and highly readable work *The History and Social Influence of the Potato.*

Although some credit is due to Gerard for being the first to mention the potato in print, he must also take the blame for the persistent myth that it had its origin in Virginia. Why he said that it reached him from there and whether in fact it did reach him from there are matters that have been discussed at enormous length. The point is only pertinent here because the confusion that he created—which resulted in the potato being referred to as the "Virginia potato"—was compounded by a second error, the tendency to confuse the potato with the sweet potato. It is possible that this double confusion may have delayed a proper assessment of the merits of the potato in Europe. It certainly was a long time before the potato became established in continental Europe, though it was quickly adopted in Ireland.

There is—or was—in Germany a statue erected in honor of Sir Francis Drake with an inscription saying that it was he who introduced the potato to Europe, in 1580. That is one legend. Another is that ships of the Spanish Armada, wrecked off the Irish coast in 1588, were carrying potatoes and that some of these washed ashore. A third, more plausible tale gives credit to Sir Walter Raleigh for having the first potatoes planted in Ireland, on his estate at Youghal in County Cork. Redcliffe Salaman found some evidence that seems to support this idea, although most historians have dismissed it as merely one more myth. I was at Youghal myself recently and conferred with local antiquarians, present-day potato growers, and anyone else who might be able to shed light on the matter. Like so many things Irish, tales of its origin there seem to abound in puzzles and apparent contradictions, and I departed none the wiser—except that I had seen for myself how well adapted County Cork is to the potato, and while there I had eaten some of the most delicious potatoes I have ever had.

Alfred Crosby, in his brilliant book *The Columbian Exchange*, joins Salaman in offering convincing reasons why the potato was adopted so rapidly in Ireland that within a few decades it had become not *a* but *the* staple food. The fact is that food was in short supply and most crops were vulnerable to destruction in war. The potato, safely underground, could not so easily be destroyed. It was fast-growing, prolific, filling, and nourishing, and conditions in Ireland were ideal for its cultivation. In the face of these advantages, any prejudices that might have existed against it were quickly overcome.

The lesson to be drawn from this is surely that if a new food from America appeared, perhaps only by chance, in the right place at the right time, it could be adopted almost at once, while in other, less favorable circumstances it could languish for centuries without being exploited. As Crosby points out, the progress of the potato in Europe was from west to east; its popularity on the Continent followed its success in the British Isles and typically occurred only in response to the powerful stimulus of desperate need or governmental intervention. In Germany, Frederick the Great urged its cultivation. In Hungary, the government ordered potatoes to be grown after a famine in 1772. In France, the potato was served at the royal table, Marie Antoinette decked herself in potato flowers, and Parmentier, whose name is commemorated in a famous potato dish, labored hard to popularize it.

The history of the potato in the Netherlands, which then included what is now Belgium, was elucidated in an essay by the Dutch food historian Joop Witteveen at the Oxford Symposium on Food History in 1983. He demonstrated that by about 1650 the potato had become established as a field crop in one part of Flanders and that it then progressed northward: to Zeeland in 1697, to Utrecht in 1731, to Overijssel in 1746, and finally to Friesland—famous to this day for its potatoes—by 1765. Expansion was most marked in the latter part of the eighteenth century, after the harsh winter of 1740, which caused high prices and famine all over Europe, and after two outbreaks of rinderpest in the Netherlands that caused a scarcity of meat and meat products.

Witteveen also furnished a fascinating analysis of the evolution of potato cookery in the Netherlands in the seventeenth and eighteenth centuries. I know of no comparable survey for any other country. For present purposes, I will simply mention that various ways of cooking the potato were already current in the seventeenth century; that the potato did not appear in the Dutch national dish—a hotpot of potatoes, carrots, and other ingredients—until 1794, around the time

13

when the Netherlands became a vassal state of France; and that it was not until the 1830s that the potato finally won a prominent place in the diet of the well-to-do.

During the nineteenth century, cultivation of the potato climbed steeply in other parts of western Europe, and in central and eastern Europe as well. Russia came last. Only in the latter half of the century, after two famines, did the potato really take off there, but by 1900 Russia was among the world's leading producers of potatoes.

Thus the general picture that emerges is that the potato required a catalyst to become popular. In particular, it tended to establish itself where food was short—often in the wake of a famine—because it produces so much in the way of calories, and so quickly too, from small plots of land. Wherever human exigencies have given it a chance to display its virtues, it has stayed on as a dietary staple.

In recent decades, much research and thought have been given to the broad question of the cultural adoption of unfamiliar foods. To relate all this to the tale I have been telling would take another essay or perhaps a book, but one observation seems pertinent here: the complex history of New World foods' reception in Europe suggests that the adoption of foods—not as fads but as integral parts of the national diet—is an area of human experience about which it is exceptionally difficult to make sound predictions. Columbus and his fellow voyagers brought back many culinary surprises to Europe and Asia, but no less surprising, at least in retrospect, are the destinies these foods were to have in the kitchens of the Old World.

CHAPTER 2

The Renaissance of Amaranth

DANIEL K. EARLY

About twenty-five years ago, alarmed by the shrinking diversity of the modern diet, University of Michigan nutritionist John Robinson embarked on a study of traditional foods the world over. Comparing archaeological evidence of prehistoric diets to known diets of contemporary hunter-gatherers, he found that dietary diversity was severely reduced when people adopted a settled agricultural way of life. Moreover, when the orientation of agriculture turned from subsistence to cash crops, he found that food diversity dwindled still more, with farmers tending to focus on a few major crops demanded by urban markets such as maize (corn), wheat, and rice.

Since this loss of diversity has adversely affected human health, particularly in the young, Dr. Robinson began a search for traditional foods that might be reintegrated into "modern" diets. After an exhaustive study of food samples from throughout the world, he concluded that amaranth, a little-known American crop, was one of thirty foods offering the greatest promise for improving human nutrition. Amaranth is a strikingly beautiful and easy-to-grow plant that bears dense clusters of tiny red, green, or purple flowers atop its central stalk and at the ends of its branches. Both the small, saucer-shaped seeds produced by these flowerheads and the plant's green or purple leaves are tasty and of high nutritional value. In fact, the seeds of domesticated species contain about 16 percent protein—more than is found in wheat, rice, or maize—and the quality of the protein is excellent, on a par with cow's milk. Amaranth leaves, which are lance-like in shape and about two inches long, compare favorably to spinach in nutritive worth and are especially rich in calcium and vitamin A.

Yet large food companies that Robinson contacted turned a deaf ear to his idea. Finally, despairing of its acceptance, in 1972 he presented his data to Robert Rodale, the publisher of *Organic Gardening* magazine and a pioneer in promoting healthier ways of life for urbanized Americans. The visionary Rodale grasped amaranth's potential, and in 1974 he made developing amaranth the top priority of his Organic Gardening and Farming Research Center.

The Rodale researchers had many questions to answer. How was amaranth traditionally planted and prepared? To what extent was it still being grown? How much genetic diversity was left? These questions ran through my mind on a warm day in August 1977 as I bounced along the roads of Mexico City in a cramped minibus headed toward the district of San Gregorio Atlapulco, where a nutritionist had told me amaranth was still grown. As an anthropologist familiar with Nahuatl peasant agriculture, I had been called on to conduct an ethnobotanical expedition to find the remaining niches where, despite foreign conquest and four hundred years of brutal subjugation, native farmers tenaciously continued their ancient tradition, preserving the green treasure of amaranth for humankind.

As I stepped out of the bus, before me lay an expanse of emerald-green canals with plots of dark, rich earth filled with flowers, chilies, and maize—the famed *chinampas*, the "floating gardens" of Mexico. These beautiful canals, now protected by government edict, are the remnant of an extensive network of waterways that once provided the Aztec capital with food. Mexico City has engulfed the area, making it an oasis amidst the city's urban expanse.

At first the *chinamperos* were suspicious and said that no one grew amaranth anymore, but after I showed the farmers an issue of *Organic Gardening* featuring amaranth and explained that fourteen thousand campesinos in the United States were trying to grow it as part of Rodale's Reader Research Project, they became very helpful. Yes, they said, there was one man who might have a patch, and they gave me directions to the nearby home of Amado García.

Amado, a lean, spry man in his early thirties, greeted me warmly, his smile, jet black hair, and dark eyes reflecting his Aztec ancestry. Half an hour later, having followed him on a circuitous route through lush plots and verdant canals, I stood filled with awe and gratitude as Amado displayed the amaranth seedlings growing in his canal-side plot. Here, surrounded by Mexico City, the cordial, part-time farmer and factory worker still raised this crop of his Aztec forebears on ground his family has cultivated continuously since before the Spanish conquest.

Amaranth itself has still deeper roots in the culture of this land. The earliest evidence of a domesticated species comes from Richard MacNeish's excavations in Tehuacán Puebla, Mexico, where he uncovered domesticated amaranth 5,500 years old. By that time, seasonally migrating family bands appear to have begun a shift from hunting and gathering to gardening such that by 5,000 years ago these family bands had achieved summer cultivation of squash, chili peppers, and amaranth. This modest beginning, contributing an estimated 6 percent of their food supply, set the stage for the development of a full-scale agriculture. Over the next millennium and a half, their output more than doubled, eventually yielding 14 percent of their food, and these family groups extended amaranth cultivation to spring planting and began domesticating maize, beans, and gourds.

Two species of grain amaranth, *Amaranthus cruentus* and *Amaranthus hypochondriacus*, were first brought under cultivation in Mesoamerica, while *Amaranthus caudatus* was independently bred in the Andes. The genius of the native plant breeders becomes evident when one compares the wild amaranths, which grow a foot or two high and have small black seeds, to the magnificent domesticated plants, whose large, multicolored blossoms tower more than six feet above the ground and yield a bounty of creamy white seeds. The Spanish conquistadors were so struck with the beauty of the amaranth that they collected some seeds and carried them home to Europe to be grown as ornamentals, but they seem to have been oblivious to the plant's value for food and forage.

Amaranth's beauty is not unrelated to its food value. Studies of numerous species, including amaranth, indicate that, throughout the Americas, native breeders worked to obtain not only increased plant size and yield but also flamboyantly colorful flowers and fruits. Often these visibly pleasing plants played key roles as foods, colorants, and objects in Indian religious rituals and ceremonies. Amaranth was no exception.

Like maize, millet, and sugarcane, amaranth is an extremely efficient converter of solar energy and is thus fast growing.

It is also prolific and highly drought-resistant, so it hardly seems remarkable that it spread far and wide from its centers of domestication in Mexico and Peru, reaching fields as far south as present-day Argentina and as far north as the pueblos of the southwestern United States. At the time of the European invasion of the Americas, the most extensive cultivation of amaranth was in the high valleys of what is now central Mexico and which then lay within the Aztec state.

The Mendocino Codex, a record of Aztec society and culture dating from the sixteenth century, lists amaranth under the Nahuatl name *huautli* as one of four major crops collected as tribute throughout the empire. This document shows eighteen royal granaries for amaranth (compared to twenty-one each for beans, maize, and chia, a sage relative whose seeds are used in a refreshing drink) and indicates that amaranth was collected from each of the seventeen provinces of the empire, with the total take reaching hundreds of thousands of bushels.

At the center of this vast empire was the area Amado still tills—the garden city of Tenochtitlán, home even then to more than 200,000 people. An ingenious system of high-yielding, sustainable aqua-agriculture based on the chinampas supported this extensive pre-industrial urban population. Other cultures had similar systems (the raised fields of the Maya and the pre-Inca plots around Lake Titicaca, for example), but the Aztecs developed this technology to its fullest potential. In establishing Tenochtitlán on Lake Texcoco, they dredged the fertile mud of the lake bottom, expanding an existing chinampa system to cover more than seventy-five square miles. The productive acreage of this zone supported as many as 100,000 people, half the city's population.

Today, just as it did five hundred years ago, seepage from the surrounding canals continuously waters the rectangular chinampas, and generation upon generation of farmers like

Amado García have continued to plant huautli in their fertile soil. Amado showed me how he scoops the rich mud from the canals to form a seedbed and then uses a special long-toothed rake to slice the bed into cubes a little more than an inch on each side. He deposits a pinch of seeds into each cube and keeps it moist with the algae-rich water of the canals. After twenty days, when the plants are six to eight inches tall, he removes the small peat-pot-like squares and transplants them to nearby hillsides, freeing the chinampa for another crop. In this fashion, each plot can produce seedlings for transplanting as well as some specialty crops.

Today, growers may start as many as seven different crops a year on each chinampa. The foods they produce include amaranth, maize, beans, chili peppers, and tomatoes as well as introduced European vegetables such as cabbages, carrots, lettuce, radishes, onions, and beets. Chinampa gardeners also grow flowers such as *cempoaxóchitl*, a species of marigold still reverently placed on graves on el Día de los Muertos, the Day of the Dead, known in English as All Souls Day. The nutrient-rich canals surrounding the chinampas also support carp and *axolotl*, a large edible salamander that Mexicans consider a delicacy.

Among the Aztecs, judging by the Mendocino Codex and similar records, huautli was prized as a gourmet food. Members of the nobility ate special kinds of tamales, including one made from a mixed amaranth and maize flour and another, the *huauquiltamalli*, created from popped amaranth seeds ground into flour. *Cauhquilmolli*, a delicious sauce, was prepared from amaranth leaves. For special tortillas called *tzoallaxcalli*, popped amaranth was combined with a syrup made from the sap of maguey cactus. In Aztec markets, vendors sold three varieties of tortillas made from amaranth flour and two amaranth drinks made from popped and ground amaranth seeds. Aztec healers used both the seeds and the leaves of amaranth to treat a number of ailments, although it is not clear from the original sources exactly what those ailments were.

Perhaps the most significant use of Aztec grain amaranth was in religious rituals. Worshippers offered huauquitamalli, the popped-amaranth tamales, to the fire god Xiuhtecutli in an annual event called Huautamalcualiztli, the Amaranth Tamale Feast. This celebration was also known as Motlaxquian Tota, literally "Our Father the Fire Toasted to Eat," a name which equates popped huautli seeds with the deity itself. During this fiesta, amaranth tamales were eaten by the faithful and placed on graves as funerary offerings.

An even more highly charged use was in rituals involving the sacred *tzoali*, a mixture of popped amaranth seeds held together with syrup from the maguey cactus and, at times, human blood. The faithful considered this preparation the flesh of the gods. Images of at least six deities—Chicomecoatl, the goddess of crops; Xiuhtecutli, god of fire; Tlaloques, the rain god; Macuilxochilt, the flower god; Omacatl, god of feasts; and Huizilopochtli, god of war—were fabricated from *tzoali* for consumption in a communion ritual.

The most elaborate of these ceremonies, centering on the war god, were described in detail by the colonial chronicler Father José de Acosta. Two days before the feast, temple maidens began grinding amaranth seed and parched maize to make a paste bound with maguey syrup. From this they formed an image of Huitzilopochtli, using green, blue, or white beads for its eyes and grains of maize for its teeth. After the Aztec lords of Tenochtitlán clothed the figure in rich vestments similar to their own, young men reverently carried it in a procession out of the city, making stops in the outlying areas of Chapultepec, Tacubaya, and Coyoacán. Returning to the city, they carefully hoisted the statue on ropes to the top of the main temple, their work accompanied by the music of flutes, drums, and conch shells. In William Safford's translation, Acosta's account continues:

> Having raised it to the top of the pyramid and placed it in a little house of flowers prepared for its reception, the young men came and scattered many flowers of diverse colors, filling the whole temple with them inside and out. This done, all the maidens came forth . . . and brought from their retreat pieces of paste of toasted maize and bledos [amaranth], the same substance of which the idol itself was made, shaped like large bones. These they handed to the young men, who carried them up the steps and placed them at the foot of the idol, filling up the whole space with them. These pieces of paste they called Uitzilipúztli's [Huitzilopochtli's] bones and flesh. . . . After them came the gods and goddesses they worshipped in diverse figures dressed in the same livery, and arranging themselves around those pieces of [amaranth] paste, they performed a certain ceremony of singing and dancing over them so that they remained blest and consecrated by the flesh and bones of that idol. At the close of the ceremony and benediction of those pieces of paste regarded by them as the flesh and bones of the idol, they paid them the same veneration as to their god. Then came forth the Sacrificers and performed the sacrifice of men . . . and in this sacrifice more human victims were offered up than on other occasions. . . . On this day consecrated to the idol Uitzilipúztli it was a precept strictly obeyed in all the land not to partake of any other food than that [amaranth] paste with syrup, of which the idol was

made, and this food had to be eaten just after break
of day, and no water could be drunk nor anything else
upon it until after midday.

When these ceremonies, dances, and sacrifices had
been concluded . . . the priests and dignitaries of the
temple took the idol of [amaranth] paste and divested
it of those adornments with which it was dressed, and
they broke it into many fragments as they did the pieces
of consecrated paste, and beginning with the seniors in
rank they distributed them, and administered them like
communion to all the people little and big, men and
women, who received them with great reverence, fear,
and tears (which was a wonder), saying that they were
eating the flesh and bones of god, and held themselves
unworthy of it. Those who were ill begged for pieces
and they were carried to them with much reverence
and veneration. All the communicants were obliged to
give a contribution (diezmo) of that seed of which the
idol was made.

The astonishment Father Acosta barely manages to contain in
this account constitutes a relatively benign response to such
rituals. More typical, it seems, was the revulsion expressed by
Juan Ruiz de Alarcón in a seventeenth-century description of
a ceremony marking the amaranth harvest. Again quoting a
translation from Safford:

Where there is manifestly a formal practice of idolatry
is at the close of the rainy season, with the first fruits of
a seed smaller than a mustard, which they call huauhtli,
for also the devil wishes the first fruits to be offered to
him. This seed is the earliest to ripen, hardening and

maturing before any other. . . . Of this seed they make a drink like gruel for drinking cold, and they also make certain dumplings (bollos) of it which in their language they call tzoalli, and these they eat cooked like their tortillas.

The idolatry consists in giving thanks for its having ripened. Of the first seed which they gather, well ground and made into paste, they make certain idols with human shape, a quarter of a yard, more or less, in size. For the day on which they are made they have prepared a quantity of their wine [pulque, fermented from the sap of the agave] and the idols having been made and cooked, they put them in their oratories, as though placing some sacred image, and putting candles and incense before them, they offer up among bouquets of flowers some of the wine prepared for the dedication. . . ; and for all this all those unite of that party, which is the fraternity of Beelzebub, and seated in a circle with much applause, the calabashes [of pulque] and bouquets placed before the said idols, there begins in their honor and praise, and in that of the devil, the music of the Teponaztli, which is a drum entirely of wood, and with it is accompanied the singing of the old people, and when they have finished their wonted drumming and singing, the patrons of the feast and the other principals of the ceremony arrive, and as a sign of sacrifice they pour out the wine contained in the calabashes, a part or the whole of it, before the little idols of Huautli, and this ceremony they call Tlatotoyahua; and then they all begin to drink what is left in the said calabashes and then they fall upon the jars of pulque until they are exhausted and their reason as well, winding up with what usually follows idolatrous ceremonies and debauches. However, the owners of the idols keep them with care for the following day, when all of those assisting at the feast in the said oratory, divide the idols into pieces, as for relics, and eat them all up.

This ritual horrified Alarcón and other Spaniards, who interpreted it as a diabolical form of the Catholic Eucharist. In discussing the first-fruits ritual, Alarcón writes, "in that which I have just related will be seen so vividly emulated and imitated the most singular mystery of the most Holy Sacrament of the Altar, in which our Lord, summing up the benefits of our Redemption ordained that most truly we should eat him; and the devil, ape-like, enemy of all good, contrives a way for these wretches to eat him, or to let themselves become possessed of him by eating him in those idols."

No historical evidence has been found that the Spaniards prohibited the cultivation of amaranth itself, but they certainly waged a repressive campaign against this "idolatry," in which amaranth played a central role. In 1525 the Church began a systematic campaign to stamp out any vestiges of pre-Columbian religious practice, and six years later a zealous bishop claimed to have destroyed twenty thousand idols and five hundred shrines. Not only idols and shrines were destroyed. Traditional worshippers were whipped, sentenced to labor for monasteries, or executed outright.

European diseases like smallpox, measles, and typhus, along with brutal exploitation of the native people on *encomienda* land grants, seriously decreased the Indian population, reducing it from an estimated 11 million in 1519 to around 6.5 million in 1540. Despite this cultural devastation, in 1577 an imperial inquiry listed amaranth among the four most common food crops grown over much of Mexico, and the amaranth rituals persisted until at least that time, for Father Acosta did not arrive to observe them until 1570.

Another Spanish survey taken in the 1890s, however, makes no mention of amaranth at all. It remains a mystery why this staple of Aztec civilization had virtually disappeared by this date. Even more complete than its disappearance as a food crop was the elimination of its place in Mesoamerican culture. In the late 1800s, the plant researcher Dr. Edward Palmer found a single *"rosario de suale,"* a *"tzoali* rosary," in a village near Guadalajara. It was made of the same amaranth paste that had been used to fabricate the Aztec deities, but no other physical evidence is left of amaranth's ancient sacred role.

Today, the main use of amaranth is in making a snack called *alegrías*, joy bars. To prepare the candies, villagers pop the seeds on a hot, dry clay griddle, or *comal*, similar to the one used for making tortillas, and bind the popped seeds with molasses, compressing and cutting this sticky mixture into little squares. Family members sell alegrías in Mexico City parks, and they are now found in Mexican health-food stores as well.

These delicious treats, so similar in manufacture to the sacred *tzoali* images of old, are not the only vestiges of amaranth's Aztec past. In the state of Morelos, south of Mexico City, I found farmers planting large fields of amaranth to supply alegría makers in Mexico City and to use themselves for amaranth flour, or *pinole*, grinding the popped seeds by hand with the *mano* and *metate*, the pre-Hispanic hand mortar and pestle. Like their Aztec ancestors, the people of Morelos take amaranth or maize pinole with them to eat on journeys, and some mix amaranth flour with water to make *atole*, a beverage reminiscent of the *michiatolli* "soft drink" once sold in the Tenochtitlán market. Some villagers in the area make tamales from amaranth flour, as do women in a few villages of the

Chiconcuac–Lake Texcoco area on the outskirts of Mexico City. Here special tamales called *cuales* are prepared on the most holy Christian feast days. They consist of a ball of bean paste covered with amaranth flour.

Farther from Mexico City, in the eastern Sierra Madre mountains of Veracruz, I met Don Cornelio Cano, a Nahuatl farmer who grows maize, beans, chili peppers, squash, and amaranth to feed his family. Don Cornelio practices traditional slash-and-burn agriculture on tropical hillsides, cutting down the brush, burning the field, and planting as soon as the ashes are cool. In fertile areas of his maize plot, he tosses some amaranth seeds, and after the young plants emerge, he picks tender handfuls to cook as potherbs called *quelites*. In picking the young plants to use as vegetables, he is also thinning the patch to allow the remaining amaranth to grow for grain. When the crop is mature, Don Cornelio harvests most of the amaranth but leaves a few stalks to drop their seeds, thus naturally reseeding the plot for a second planting.

In the Andes—the other great center of amaranth domestication—Indians of the Quechua culture have grown *Amaranthus caudatus* for many centuries, using methods as inventive as those of Don Cornelio, Amado García, and other Aztec descendants to the north. Modern-day Quechua farmers of Bolivia, Peru, and Ecuador practice a high-altitude agriculture that once supported the vast Inca civilization. Although they are best known for giving the world the potato, the ancient Andean farmers domesticated a host of other valuable plants as well—three high-protein grains, a wealth of nutritious tubers, and a hardy, protein-rich seed of a lupine known as *tarwi* (*Lupinus mutabilis*).

Unfortunately, the Incas left few written records, and historical information on the role of amaranth in the Inca civilization is lacking. We can surmise that *kiwicha*, as the Quechua call the grain, held less cultural significance than did the Aztec species. Maize rather than amaranth was the Incas' ritual food, and quinoa was their basic grain. Nevertheless, amaranth culture has persisted in small-scale subsistence farming to the present day.

In 1985 I went to Cuzco, the ancient Inca capital, to study traditional Quechua methods of amaranth cultivation and use. Thirty-five years earlier, Jonathan Sauer's reports had indicated that amaranth was then a marginal crop and that its cultivation in the Andes was declining. I was not reassured when Professor Sumar Kalinowski, director of the Amaranth Project at the Center for Andean Crops, informed me that very few peasants grew amaranth anymore.

To ensure survival in the harsh Andean environment, Quechua farmers grow a wide variety of crops in a range of ecological zones all over the mountainsides. My research for the ensuing six months was therefore analogous to looking for a needle in a haystack. Like an agricultural Dick Tracy, I bussed and hiked the southern Andes, flashing color photographs at farmers and asking if they had ever seen this plant.

Little by little I discovered that *Amaranthus caudatus* is still being sparsely but widely grown and that its genetic diversity remains intact. In remote hamlets in central and northern Peru, some Quechua farmers cultivate the old crop on small plots in the maize-growing zone between 8,100 and 10,500 feet. Also, in the jungles of southeastern Peru some farmers cultivate amaranth on a small scale, using slash-and-burn techniques.

The highland Quechua farmers generally intercrop amaranth with other grains, principally maize and quinoa. Intercropping, as organic farmers elsewhere have confirmed, helps protect plants against disease and predators, and the Quechua long ago developed a number of sophisticated intercropping patterns. These have been passed down for centuries so that contemporary Quechua farmers distinguish at least four basic patterns and in any particular field may utilize them and variants of them in an almost infinite number of ways.

Like their counterparts in Mexico, Quechua families pop amaranth seeds, generally using a special clay pot, or *tostador*, which is also used for roasting quinoa. To prevent the seeds from burning, they are stirred with a spatula shaped like a drumstick. Villagers eat the popped seeds directly, and some consider them a tonic for the elderly, but mainly they are used for making *turrones*, amaranth balls similar to the Mexican alegrías, made by mixing the popped seeds with molasses. Quechua women sell turrones in local markets and even, at times, in the modern capital of Lima.

For a breakfast food, families prepare an amaranth flour called *mash'ka*, similar to the Mexican pinole, grinding the popped seeds with implements much like the Mexican mortar and pestle. Villagers also ferment amaranth seeds to make *chicha*, a native beer that is consumed socially and used ritually as an offering to Mother Earth before planting. One farmer explained to me: "One must give the earth one or two drops of *chicha*. *Pochatierra* is the earth. Because the earth exists. It has life, they say. So does the *chicha*."

In the Huancavalica area of Peru, peasants use the plant's stalk for its high calcium content. After harvesting the seedheads, they burn the stalks and later mix the ash with water, using this to soak maize to prepare it for making tamale dough. Some growers in this area also shape the ash into hard balls about an inch in diameter that are sold locally for use as adjuncts in chewing coca leaves, an ancient tradition in the Andes. Villagers scrape the ball with their teeth as they chew the leaves, and the calcium in the amaranth ash releases the alkaloids in the leaves, enhancing the coca's effect as a mild stimulant.

Both in southern Peru and in Ecuador, Quechua people cultivate certain wild amaranths to use their bright flowers for healing and ritual. Peruvian families of the Cuzco region treat toothache and fevers with a tea brewed from the blossoms of an amaranth known as *airampo* (*Amaranthus hybridus*). Villagers in Ecuador relish *draque*, a potent alcoholic beverage made by boiling the flowers of *Amaranthus hybridus* and adding the resulting vividly red infusion to aguardiente rum. Draque afficionados say it "purifies the blood" and helps restore the regularity of menstrual cycles.

Amaranth also has a number of applications at festival time. During Carnival, Quechua women boil the red petals and add the infusion to chicha to give it an enticing color. Sometimes before dancing they paint their cheeks, using the red flowers as rouge, or while dancing carry bundles of amaranth in shawls on their backs like little babies, with the bright blooms sticking out where the baby's face would be. During el Día de los Muertos, Ecuadorians celebrate by eating *pan de finados*, specially baked breads shaped in animal or human forms, and wash this down with *colada morada*, a drink made from maize flour colored with amaranth flower infusion.

In general, Quechua methods of amaranth cultivation, preparation, and use bear strong similarities to Aztec practices, probably because innovators in the two areas found parallel solutions to the challenges this unusual plant presents. Not all their solutions are the same, however, and opportunities exist for transferring time-tested indigenous techniques. For example, the Aztec method of stirring the seeds with a whisk is much more efficient than the Andean drumstick method. When my wife and I suggested this simple change to Quechua women in the Cuzco area, it was readily accepted.

Amaranth is making a comeback in both Peru and Mexico. Alan García, who had just been elected to the presidency of Peru when I arrived there, surprised his nation by inviting mothers from the *"pueblos jovenes,"* the shantytowns ringing Lima, to be guests of honor at his first presidential banquet. Another surprise was that the banquet featured Andean foods, including amaranth cookies for dessert. In addition, President García asked Professor Kalinowski, my mentor at the Center for Andean Crops, to direct a national amaranth campaign to stimulate the production and use of kiwicha throughout the country. The campaign received widespread publicity, and suddenly almost everyone, it seemed, was talking about amaranth. The plant gained a new status, transformed from an almost forgotten "poor people's food" into a symbol of national pride.

In Mexico in 1986, the eminent agronomist Dr. Alfredo Marroquín invited peasant growers, along with national and international experts, to the First National Amaranth Seminar, stimulating excitement about amaranth among specialists and the general public alike. When I visited amaranth-producing villages a year after the conference, alegría makers were eagerly passing around photocopies of the proceedings, the originals having already sold out. Amaranth growers in the state of Tlaxcala told me about the high amino acid content of their amaranth and how nutritious it was for their children. The governors of Tlaxcala and nearby Querétaro followed up, each holding outstanding state conferences to promote amaranth, again melding the expertise of peasant growers with that of national and international specialists.

To channel the rising interest in amaranth, in 1988 Roman

Millan, an amaranth promoter, formed the Huautli Institute in Mexico City to support research into amaranth cultivation, product manufacturing, and marketing. Among the commercial projects currently underway is an exciting venture headed by Dr. Marroquín and architect Eugenio Negrete to build a pilot plant to produce amaranth grain, protein concentrate, and starch. Particles of amaranth starch are extremely fine, their diameter averaging just one micron, which makes the starch ideal for industrial applications in cosmetics and film.

In the United States, the Rodale group has continued to lead the way in amaranth development. Skip Kauffman, director of Rodale's Research and Development Center, and his colleague, agronomist Leon Weber, have bred amaranth varieties suited for mechanized U.S. agriculture, and under their tutelage, U.S. growers have had success with the crop. In eastern Colorado, Wyoming, and Nebraska, golden fields of wheat have now been joined by towering heads of crimson, violet, and green amaranth gently waving in the breeze. Over the last decade, land in production has grown from nothing to over two thousand acres. Amaranth's drought-resistant properties make it an especially attractive alternative to dryland wheat in the northern tier of the western states.

Ed Hubbard, an enthusiastic amaranth advocate, has taken matters a step further by forming the American Amaranth Institute to educate farmers and the food industry about amaranth and to develop the market for amaranth in the United States. Many small bakeries are now turning out amaranth bread, cookies, and other products for local consumption, and the grain is moving swiftly into the mainstream health-food market. Arrowhead Mills produces amaranth flour and apple amaranth granola, while Health Valley is manufacturing amaranth cereal, pasta, cookies, graham crackers, and even pilaf.

The big surprise in the spread of amaranth comes from

China. In 1982, Dr. Yue Shaoxian of the Institute of Crop Breeding and Cultivation visited the Rodale Research Center and carried back to Beijing several pounds of the Rodale-improved seed. She subsequently reported that sixty researchers across the vast Chinese countryside are working with amaranth and that by 1987 Chinese farmers had more than 177,000 acres of amaranth under cultivation. Much of this goes for livestock and poultry forage, but amaranth is also marrying into Chinese cultural traditions in the form of a nutritious, naturally dark soy sauce consisting of 15 percent dark-seeded amaranth and 85 percent soy beans.

Amaranth has also spread to Africa, where Dr. V. K. Gupta of the University of Nairobi has developed high-yielding, drought-resistant lines of amaranth that are gaining acceptance among local farmers. Skip Kauffman informs me that Dr. Gupta created new lines by crossing seeds that I brought back from Amado García's village in 1975, so the germplasm that Amado and his ancestors had been cultivating for centuries is now helping to feed people in drought-stricken Africa.

Amaranth's resurgence has been expedited by the dedicated work of researchers and commercial growers, but if it regains its place as a major dietary staple, our greatest debt will be to people like Don Cornelio and Amado García and to the generations of native farmers before them who, despite brutal conquest and continuing exploitation, resolutely kept on planting kiwicha and huautli, preserving for humanity this precious resource.

CHAPTER 3

Vanilla: Nectar of the Gods

PATRICIA RAIN

Most of us can immediately identify the delicate, seductive scent of the amber liquid in the small brown bottle. Even those unfamiliar with pure vanilla extract certainly know the subtle taste of vanilla ice cream and are aware of vanilla's use as a flavoring in many other foods. Indeed, though it has only been available as an extract for about a hundred years, vanilla is now so commonplace that its name serves generically to indicate things that are plain or ordinary.

For all its uses and its wide acceptance in Western society, vanilla has an extraordinary, little-known story. It comes from the fruit of a tropical vine of the Orchidaceae, or orchid family, the largest family of flowering plants in the world. Of the more than 35,000 orchid species that botanists have described, only vanilla orchids produce edible fruit, and only two of the fifty vanilla orchid species have commercial value, *Vanilla planifolia* and *Vanilla tahitensis*. In fact, the latter, better known as Tahitian vanilla, is a twentieth-century, laboratory-bred cousin of the older plant, so the story really begins with a single unusual evolutionary development in the realm of flowering plants.

Although members of the orchid family are found all over the world, vanilla orchids are indigenous to the rainforests of the Caribbean, Central America, the southeastern coast of Mexico, and the northernmost latitudes of South America. The vines are now grown around the world in moist tropical lands that lie within twenty-five degrees of the equator. Vanilla prefers altitudes of less than 2,000 feet and an equal mixture of sun and shade, such as it receives in the tree canopy of its native habitat. It grows best where ten months of moderate rainfall are followed by a two-month dry season, which stimulates flowering and fruiting. This highly specialized plant does not tolerate extended droughts and favors gently sloping ground that prevents water from rotting its root system in the jungle floor.

If allowed to grow freely, vanilla vines climb high into the forest canopy, drawing some of their nourishment through aerial roots that grip the host trees. The orchid's satiny, greenish-yellow flower appears in clusters of twenty or more, suspended on short stalks that sprout from the stem of the vine. Buds take as long as six weeks to mature, then open for only one day, blooming in the morning, beginning to wilt by early afternoon, and usually dropping off by nightfall unless they have been pollinated. A vine may produce as many as a thousand blossoms, but even on a commercial vanilla plantation, at most three hundred of these are pollinated and develop into fruit.

The fruit takes the form of slender cylindrical pods, often referred to as beans due to their resemblance to string beans. Pods grow to lengths of four to twelve inches and are harvested when, after eight or nine months, their tips turn yellow. If allowed to ripen fully on the vine, the beans take on a golden hue and eventually split open to release thousands of tiny seeds.

Interestingly, neither the vanilla flower nor its fruit has a conspicuous scent or flavor; only after the pod has fermented does vanillin, the chemical compound primarily responsible for its delightful fragrance and taste, become readily discernible. This biochemical fact makes it remarkable that, in antiquity, vanilla's virtues were discovered, let alone that an efficient means of curing the beans was developed and the plant itself brought under intensive cultivation.

The people credited with all these accomplishments are the Totonacs, who still survive in the Gulf coast region of their ancestors, in the modern Mexican state of Veracruz. At least a thousand years ago the Totonacs worked out a means of processing the beans very much like the methods used today in commercial vanilla extraction, and they began to make vanilla an integral part of their culture. In addition to using it as a perfume and as a flavoring for food and drink, the Totonacs found that vanilla was effective as a medicine, an aphrodisiac, and an insect repellent.

Not surprisingly, the Totonacs gave both the vanilla bean, which they called *tlilxochitl*, and the orchid, *xanath*, major places in their religion and culture. According to Totonac myth, when the world was fresh and still frequented by deities, a beautiful young goddess, Xanath, visited the Earth and fell in love with a Totonac warrior. As a goddess—indeed, daughter of the great goddess who ensured fertility—Xanath could not marry a mortal, but neither could she bring herself to abandon him. She ultimately resolved her predicament by bestowing herself upon her lover and his people in the form of the first vanilla vine. The blossoming and fruiting of this heavenly plant, so runs the myth, would provide the Totonacs a source of eternal happiness.

Rather than leaving this gift to chance, Totonac farmers learned to husband the vine to great advantage. They found they could increase not only the accessibility but also the output of the vines by preventing them from growing high into the trees. As long as a vanilla vine is growing directly upward, it will not flower, and the higher it climbs, the more energy it diverts from flowering to leaf production. Thus the Totonacs looped each vine back to the ground once it reached a five-foot height on the host tree.

They also discovered that they could increase the vine's productivity by hand-pollinating the flowers. Male and female parts of the vanilla orchid are separated by a membranous tissue that prevents the flowers from self-pollinating. In its native habitat, vanilla's reproductive needs are met by a few species of ants and hummingbirds and the tiny melipona bee, but since its blossoms last less than a day, the number of flowers fertilized tends to be low. The Totonacs ensured a high rate of pod production by performing the "marriage of vanilla," as the pollination process is known.

About five hundred years before the arrival of the conquistadors, the Aztecs subjugated the coastal Indian tribes and thereafter required the Totonacs to surrender a portion of their annual vanilla harvest as tribute. Although the Totonacs chafed under Aztec domination, they were in no position to resist the powerful empire until Hernán Cortés arrived in 1520, at which point the Totonacs joined forces with the Tlaxcalan Indians to assist in his march on Tenochtitlán, the Aztec capital.

Aztec prophesies foretold the arrival of fair-skinned, blond-haired gods from the east, so the Aztec ruler, Moctezuma, initially greeted Cortés and his troops with deference rather than with the armed resistance that the Spaniards had anticipated. Among the honors accorded Cortés and his officers were offerings of *chocolatl*, the drink of Aztec royalty, made from ground cacao and maize sweetened with honey and flavored with *tlilxochitl*—a recipe noted in the meticulously kept journals of Bernal Díaz del Castillo, an observant and educated soldier accompanying Cortés. Despite the warm reception, Cortés ruthlessly subjugated the Aztecs, succeeding in part because an epidemic of smallpox, brought by the invaders, so devastated the native population that it could not effectively resist his forces.

Cortés's thanks for the services of the Totonacs was to double their taxes. Evidently he and his officers had quickly developed an appetite for their product, but it is unclear whether Cortés carried vanilla back to Spain on this or later voyages. Along with indigo, cochineal dyes, and cacao, vanilla had been introduced to Europe in 1510 by Spanish colonists, probably people based in Cuba who had made exploratory forays throughout the Caribbean region. Apparently they knew vanilla only as a perfume, however, so it was left to Cortés and others to report its use as a flavoring. Some accounts credit Bernardino de Sahagún, a Franciscan friar who went to Mexico in 1529, for first instructing Europeans in the uses of *tlilxochitl* through his *Florentine Codex: General History of the Things of New Spain*, published in Spain in 1560.

However it transpired, vanilla soon rose to popularity in Spain as a flavoring agent, and Spanish factories were producing vanilla-flavored chocolate powder by the latter half of the sixteenth century. Like many of the exotic spices from distant lands, vanilla was so rare and expensive that only Europe's royalty and wealthiest classes could obtain it. King Philip II of Spain reportedly enjoyed a drink of chocolate laced with vanilla as a nightcap, but the ingredients were in such short supply that even he had to accept rationing.

In 1571, King Philip dispatched Francisco Hernández to

Mexico on a six-year mission during which Hernández studied vanilla and other elements of the New World pharmacopoeia. In his work *Rerum Medicarum Novae Hispaniae Thesaurus*, published in Rome in 1651, he identified the plant as *Araco aromaico* and noted that the Indians used the fruit not only for its pleasant taste and fragrance but also for its healing properties.

In the meantime, the French botanist Carolus Clusius had described vanilla in 1605 under the name *Lobus oblongus aromaticus*, based on a sample of untreated beans he had received from Hugh Morgan, apothecary to Queen Elizabeth I. Clusius commented that the pods smelled like benzoin and that their fumes were strong enough to provoke headaches. Presumably the specimens had begun to ferment and decompose before they came into his hands.

The word *vaynilla* finally entered the botanical literature in 1658, when William Piso prepared a report on Spanish uses of the bean. This word, from which the genus took both its common and scientific names, was a diminutive form of *vaina*, meaning a little sheath, scabbard, or pod. *Vaina* comes, in turn, from the Latin word *vagina*, whose first meaning also is sheath. Curiously, the Greek word *orchis*, which is the root of *orchid*, means testicle. Given these etymologies and the fact that both the Aztecs and the Europeans of Renaissance times considered vanilla a powerful aphrodisiac, it might be wise to treat the contents of that benign-looking bottle on the pantry shelf as something more than just a flavoring.

For food purposes, vanilla was regarded as an adjunct to chocolate until 1602, when Hugh Morgan, the British apothecary, suggested that it be used as a flavoring in its own right. This proposal evidently pleased the throne, for Queen Elizabeth became an extraordinary devotee of vanilla, in her later years allegedly consuming only food and drink enlivened with its flavor. The Spaniards, after relishing vanilla for a while as a flavoring for chocolate, eventually cast it aside in favor of cinnamon. Not so the French. They became thoroughly enamored of vanilla, and by the eighteenth century it was used more heavily in France than in any other European country— as a flavoring for chocolate, confections, and ices and as a scent for perfumes and tobaccos.

To support this national habit and to reduce its cost, the French shipped Mexican vanilla cuttings to the Bourbon Islands (now Madagascar, Réunion, and the Comoro Islands) and their other tropical colonies, thus becoming probably the primary agents for dispersion of the species outside the New World. Cuttings were successfully established in the French holdings by 1730, but the vines seldom flowered and, lacking natural pollinators, never produced fruit. A rumor circulated that Moctezuma had cursed the plant such that it would never bear outside its native habitat.

This failure preserved Mexico's—and the Totonacs'—grip on the world vanilla trade for more than a century, until 1837, when a Belgian scientist named Charles Moren traveled into the Mexican rainforest to study the botany of the vanilla orchid and Totonac methods of cultivation. The Totonacs had proved shrewd not only as agriculturists but also as merchants, driving hard bargains and controlling vanilla production to keep prices high. The end of their lucrative monopoly was assured in 1841, however, when Edmund Albius, a former slave from Réunion, followed up Moren's findings by perfecting a vanilla pollination technique. Albius's method, employing a slender bamboo stylus, remains in use today, most of the labor being performed by dexterous women and children.

Vanilla plantations soon flourished in the Bourbon Islands and in Mauritius, the Seychelles, Tahiti, Ceylon, Java, the Philippines, the West Indies, and parts of Africa. Vanilla was also planted successfully in India and China but never became a commercial enterprise there. By the end of the nineteenth century, more vanilla was produced in tropical Asia and Madagascar than in Mexico.

According to Waverly Root's encyclopedic book *Food*, vanilla took hold in the United States through a French connection. It seems that Thomas Jefferson discovered vanilla while posted in Paris as the U.S. ambassador, and in 1789, after returning to Philadelphia (then the national capital) to serve as secretary of state, he found himself craving it. A Frenchman in Jefferson's employ was dispatched to buy vanilla beans, only to find that no one in the city knew what they were. Jefferson ordered fifty of the precious pods from Paris and presumably educated his friends and others to the delights of the aromatic fruit. A few decades later, in the early nineteenth century, Dolley Madison served vanilla ice cream at a presidential dinner, and Philadelphia soon adopted the new dessert, for many years thereafter retaining a reputation for the world's best vanilla ice cream.

In the nineteenth century, vanilla also became available in U.S. apothecary shops as a stomach sedative. A strong tincture of vanilla was made by distilling the beans with alcohol and water and adding a hefty amount of sugar. Tincture of vanilla was listed in the *American Pharmacopoeia* until 1915 and may still be found in some small pharmacies.

There is no record of when vanilla extract first appeared in grocery stores. When McCormick and Company, the world's largest purveyor of herbs and spices, was founded in 1889, vanilla was not among the flavorings that it offered, but the extract seems to have become commercially available about that time. Certainly vanilla has been known in the small brown bottles that fit well in the hand throughout most, if not all, of the twentieth century.

Today, Madagascar ranks as the chief vanilla-producing

country of the world, but its "Bourbon" beans are beginning to get a run for their money from the Tahitian species that is grown, along with the older species, in French colonies of the Pacific and in neighboring island states. Until the mid-1980s, almost all the Tahitian vanilla went directly to France, but now American importers are making purchases in places like Tonga, because the quality of Pacific vanilla is excellent. The traditional beans' advantage of a higher vanillin content is offset by the more floral scent and flavor of the Tahitian beans, attributed to their greater concentrations of pipernol and heliotropine, two of the other 150 chemical compounds that have been identified in vanilla. One species ought not be considered better or worse than the other; they are simply different.

Meanwhile, the tropical forests of southeastern Mexico have largely been destroyed, and most of the land where vanilla once grew wild is now used to pasture cattle or for citrus production. Vanilla is still raised in the area, however, and Totonac culture is still structured around its growing cycle, with a traditional harvest festival held in late January of each year. But the Totonacs have been reduced to plantation hands, and despite their vast knowledge of both the territory and the needs of vanilla, they are struggling to keep their ancestral crop growing in a vastly altered environment.

In the past several years there has been a lot of confusion about Mexican vanilla, as tourists have returned from Caribbean vacations toting big bottles of "extract" purchased at extremely low prices. Unfortunately, most of this liquid is not vanilla. Mexico, Haiti, and other cash-poor Caribbean countries are simply trading on the region's reputation as a producer of fine vanilla. An absence of strict regulations governing the production and labeling of food and drink invites entrepreneurs to sell very different substances under the name of "pure vanilla extract," and usually what the bargain hunter gets is synthetic vanillin, derived from coal tar or paper mill by-products. It is often cut with coumarin, a potentially toxic compound that may either be extracted from the fruit of the tonka bean tree or synthesized in a chemical laboratory. Mixed together, coumarin and vanillin smell much more like the true extract than the synthetic vanillin does by itself. Red dyes are frequently added to this brew as well, and it is generally sold for about the same price per quart that pure synthetic vanillin draws in the United States. The difference is that U.S.-made synthetic vanillin is not fortified with coumarin or with the red dyes used in Mexico, both of which are banned by the U.S. Food and Drug Administration.

The best clues as to whether a bottle purporting to be vanilla is really pure vanilla extract are its price and alcohol content. If the price is less than twenty-three dollars a quart or if little or no alcohol is detectable, you are not being offered pure vanilla extract. Alcohol is always used in the extraction process, and the FDA requires that pure vanilla extract contain a minimum of 35 percent alcohol. Though the FDA maintains no specific limits on vanilla's sugar content or on other additives, it does require that they be mentioned on the label. Some U.S. companies supplement their vanilla extracts with caramel coloring and preservatives, but the finest vanilla is not adulterated in any way and is improved only by aging before it goes to market.

If, as the old adage says, imitation is the sincerest form of flattery, the profusion of pseudo-vanilla substances only goes to show the lasting appeal of the ancient Totonac preparation. Vanilla still serves as a delightful perfume and continues to have medical applications as a stomach sedative and ingredient in cough syrups. Of course, its usual place is on the kitchen shelf, and though few cooks have learned to exploit its full potential—restricting it mostly to use in desserts and flavored drinks—vanilla maintains its claim on our palates. For all the extravagant flavors of ice cream sold today, vanilla remains the favorite by a wide margin. The old American flavoring may have become ubiquitous, but it will never be plain or ordinary.

CHAPTER 4

Maize: Gift from America's First Peoples

WALTON C. GALINAT

On October 16, 1492, European eyes fell for the first time on fields of maize, the lanky grass known to science as *Zea mays* and in the United States commonly called corn. The place was Haiti, and the Europeans were crew members from the ships of Christopher Columbus. Three weeks later his exploring party in northeastern Cuba came upon advanced agriculture and a prosperous settlement whose friendly inhabitants presented them with gifts, including ears of maize.

Columbus did not realize that the gift of maize was far more valuable than the spices or gold he hoped to find. He had no way of knowing that the history of maize traced back some 8,000 years or that it represented the most remarkable plant breeding accomplishment of all time. He might have been embarrassed if he had understood that then, as now, this plant developed by peoples he judged poor and uncivilized far outstripped in productivity any of the cereals bred by Old World farmers—wheat, rice, sorghum, barley, and rye. Were he alive today, he would certainly be astonished to see the extent to which the advent of maize has affected land use, food production, cuisine, and population growth around the world.

Cereals have played a vital role in the rise and evolution of human cultures. Their dried grains can be produced in immense quantities, are relatively easy to transport, and can be kept for long periods. Their high nutritive value stems from the fact that they are seeds, housing embryos and the reserves needed to nourish a new plant as it germinates and establishes itself. They contain an array of carbohydrates, proteins, oils, vitamins, and minerals as useful in sustaining animal life as they are in fueling the growth of their own seedlings, and their consumption (directly and in the form of livestock fattened on grain) has furnished the dietary foundation for the great civilizations of both the Old World and the New.

Maize is extraordinary, even among cereals, not only for its productivity (a single ear of modern maize yields approximately a thousand large grains) but also for its advanced degree of domestication. No other cereal species has so completely lost its natural ability to disperse its seeds in the wild and thus to propagate itself without human intervention. In this and other respects, maize is the cereal whose future is most tightly bound up with humanity's; it has become a truly symbiotic partner of humankind.

The same traits that make maize so useful to us as a cereal also prevent it from surviving as a wild plant. The multiple layers of husk that enclose the ear furnish it protection on the stalk, while the dense clustering of kernels on the rigid cob makes it a very convenient package for harvesting, storage, and shelling by human hands and machines. When an ear falls to the earth and its kernels sprout, however, the competition for growing space within the mass of seedlings is so intense that none lives long enough to mature and reproduce. To put it in contemporary terms, this supremely domesticated crop suffers from an absence of the family planning ordinarily practiced by Mother Nature.

Since its future rests in our hands (and our future depends on its continued success), it is imperative that we understand maize. The essential questions to be explored are the same questions we ask about other things, from the vastness of the cosmos to the smallest of subatomic particles: Where did it come from, and where is it going? To answer the second question, we must answer the first, for the future of maize or any other species is contingent on the genetic structure and materials it has acquired through natural selection and breeding. Answers about maize's past ought to be relatively easy to find, since its history has been so greatly shaped by human hands, and if we can grasp what maize breeders did in the past, we will be able to protect its future and efficiently direct its further breeding.

The ancestor of maize is a wild grass called *teosinte* (God's corn) that still grows in some parts of Mexico, Guatemala, and Honduras. Teosinte remains highly successful in the wild, while maize fails, as I have said, due to its human-engineered hyperabundance. Teosinte, however, is all but identical with maize in its cell form and genetic structure, differing from primitive forms of maize by only a few characters. After all these thousands of years of coexistence with maize, teosinte remains fully interfertile with it, and spontaneous crosses between the two occur normally when they grow in proximity. To prevent such crosses, which would diminish the productivity of maize, people have created an artificial breeding barrier by isolating maize from teosinte. A few isolating mechanisms such as differences in flowering time have evolved in teosinte as well, protecting it from the traits it would receive through crosses with maize—traits that would decrease its viability as a wild plant.

How maize arose from teosinte has long been a subject of sharp dispute among scientists. Traditional botanists and taxonomists, who think of evolution in terms of gradual shifts in gene frequencies occurring as a consequence of natural selection, reason that the two or three gene changes separating teosinte from primitive maize should have taken millennia to transpire and that this process should have entailed intermediate forms, halfway maizes, connecting teosinte to maize. That no such intermediate stages have been located in the archaeological record poses a serious problem for proponents of this theory.

Other scientists, myself among them, hold that the genetic change in question happened quite suddenly and was a result of human intervention. A large wild population of any species carries a measure of genetic variability created by mutation. Consider the variability of our own species, for example. We may assume that each of the genes that, in combination, would transform teosinte into primitive maize had mutated many times and that the mutant forms that created maize were part of the load of variability carried in teosinte populations. If ancient Mesoamericans discerned promising traits in certain teosinte plants and then selected and isolated these plants, primitive maize would have swiftly emerged through cross-breeding, leaving scant traces in the archaeological record.

Though the first peoples of this hemisphere obviously lacked the knowledge of cytogenetics and biotechnology available today, there is every reason to believe that they possessed powers of observation and imagination equal to our own and sufficient to take this remarkable stride in plant breeding. They were thoughtful, capable people who domesticated not only maize but also numerous other plants, creating a full-fledged agriculture long before their first contact with Europeans. Their accomplishments in the fields laid the foundation for the great cities and cultures of the Aztecs, Mayas, and Incas, complex societies on a par with any that existed in the Old World.

The observation critical to the domestication and breeding of crops, East or West, is that offspring tend to resemble their parents. Armed with this intuitive understanding of inheritance and driven by experience with famine, aboriginal planters learned not to consume the best seed but to save and sow it. By another leap of imagination and perhaps as a consequence of their desire to control the areas they planted, they apparently also discovered that crops improved generation by generation if they were planted apart from wild populations—in irrigated areas in the desert, for instance, or in rainforest plots cleared by slash-and-burn methods.

These insightful but relatively simple steps would account for the segregation of maize's precursors into evolutionary pools in which the additional selection of recombinant types would complete the transformation into primitive maize. It seems obvious that the early Mesoamericans were teosinte breeders before they were corn breeders, and it should be obvious as well that the sudden appearance of maize in the archaeological record can be explained only by such human involvement in the breeding process. This was not a case of natural evolution; the human eye, mind, and hand opened the way for this genetic leap.

How could the eyes of a hungry people gathering teosinte as food overlook mutant plants that doubled and then redoubled the yield per ear? One of the changes that took place, we now know, was a mutation on the short arm of chromosome 2 that yielded four ranks of kernels where teosinte had only two. Another mutation transformed single female spikelets into paired ones, and this, together with the gain in ranks, gave the first ear of maize four times as many kernels as its teosinte progenitor. Later mutations, such as exposure and enlargement of the kernel, would also have made an appreciable difference in the appearance and usefulness of maize. Attentive native planters would have selected for these developments, which increased the productivity of the crop. Other selections, such as for permanent enclosure of the ear in husks and elongation of the styles (silks) beyond the husks for pollination, further manifest these first maize breeders' acumen and concern for increasing productivity.

If a plant is transported into isolation, a trait that has a frequency as low as one in a million in the wild may appear in every member of the offspring population, depending on its breeding behavior. A time period extending to thousands of years is not required for a major genetic change under such circumstances, as it would be if only natural evolution were operating on the species. It took only a few centuries for Europeans to breed the wild plant *Brassica oleracea*, similar to collards, into the cole crop vegetables—kale, cabbage, brussels sprouts, broccoli, kohlrabi, and cauliflower—and the change from teosinte to maize is no more dramatic than this. The development of the ear is an adaptation to a switch in the niche from wild to domestic.

While the natural distribution of teosinte has contracted within Mexico, Guatemala, and Honduras since prehistoric times, that of maize has continued to expand through human efforts to adapt it to new habitats. Starting about 8,000 years ago, primitive maize was carried from Mexico (principally from Oaxaca, Tehuacán, and the Valley of Mexico) into distant regions, especially southward through Central America and on into South America. Primitive types similar to the earliest Tehuacán maize reached Ayacucho, Peru, and apparently the eastern slopes of the Andes as early as 4,000 years ago. By the time Columbus arrived on the scene, maize had been established throughout most of continental America as well as in the Caribbean islands where he first encountered it.

The process of maize adaptation continued to unfold as it entered its many new niches, and hundreds of distinct races appeared. (Some three hundred races have been described in a series of monographs published by the National Research Council of the National Academy of Sciences.) Resourceful breeding by native peoples of the Americas resulted in maize suitable for diverse agricultural situations. For areas with short growing seasons and long days, they bred such forms as the Gaspé Flint from the Gaspé Peninsula of Canada, whose tassel is formed even in the seed, and the early-flowering Araucano Flint and Coya races from southern Chile and Argentina, respectively. The maize known as Caribbean Yellow Flint flourishes at sea level in the hot tropics, while one called Puno (Confite Puneno) is adapted for cultivation near Lake Titicaca, at an elevation of 12,000 feet, growing successfully at temperatures as low as 40°F, ten degrees below the normal threshold for maize. Another race, Chococeno, was selected for growth in uncultivated, wet areas on the west coast of Colombia, whereas Hopi and Navajo maize is adapted for deep planting in the deserts of the Southwest. Most maize fails to emerge from depths of more than four inches, but the Hopi and Navajo maize has an elongated embryonic organ (mesocotyl) that enables it to sprout to the surface from eighteen inches down, where the desert soil retains sufficient moisture to sustain its growth.

Thanks to the adaptability of the species and to their own breeding prowess, maize became the staple of the vast majority of Native American peoples. In many parts of the hemisphere, it was planted together with beans and squash, its stalk supporting the runners of the other plants, whose nutritive properties complement its own. A thousand years before Columbus, maize became the main foodstuff that powered the Aztec, Maya, and Inca civilizations, its abundance helping to create wealth and leisure and thus to stimulate a flowering of arts and crafts.

In North America, maize has played a crucial role not only in indigenous societies but also in the survival of the first English colonists, in the settlement of the West, and in the rise of the United States as a world power. In 1620, maize received from Indians allowed half of the 102 Mayflower Pilgrims to survive their first, terrible winter at Plymouth Plantation. The words of Governor Bradford, now inscribed on a brass plaque at Truro (Corn Hill) on Cape Cod, reflect the Pilgrims' gratitude: "And sure it was God's good providence that we found this corne for we know not how else we should have done."

The following year, they succeeded in growing twenty acres of maize themselves, and after an abundant harvest that fall, they held a feast with their Indian neighbors that has found its place in American folklore as the first Thanksgiving. It is perhaps no exaggeration to say that without the gift of corn from "God's good providence"—through the agency of his indigenous intermediaries—Plymouth Plantation would have failed, and the estimated fifteen million descendants of the Mayflower party would not be among us.

Maize had a similar role in ensuring the survival of the settlers at Jamestown in Virginia. Only 38 of the 105 members of the Jamestown colony lived out its first winter, and all of them would probably have perished had not Pocahontas intervened to save the life of John Smith and later bartered for maize to feed his famished compatriots. In this case, maize can be credited, if you will, for ten million people who trace their ancestry to the Jamestown settlers. Summing up this history in his paper "The Mystery of Maize," George Beadle writes: "Something like one out of ten of us in this favored nation would not have been born—had it not been for corn."

Through Columbus and the later explorers and conquistadors who came to the New World, maize passed into the fields and onto the tables of Europe, Asia, Africa, and other lands. The history of its dispersion is complex and has not yet been fully resolved, but it can be safely reported that maize was adopted with relative alacrity by the farmers and diners of the Old World. Readily recognizable as a cereal, it was less suspect than other American crops, and its high productivity, appealing taste, and ability to grow in soil and water conditions that were otherwise marginal soon made it an important contributor to the food supply, especially in Europe and Asia.

With this transfer, of course, maize breeding came into new hands as well, and the development of its genetic and agricultural possibilities continued as Old World farmers adapted the maize races they had received so as to satisfy local growing conditions and culinary preferences. Many useful modifications have been made in the great crop during the five centuries of Old World experimentation with it, and a few developments, such as Chinese "baby corn," are known worldwide, but it can be said without risk of chauvinism that the most important maize breeding achievements have continued to occur in the Americas, where the genetic diversity of maize is at its zenith.

The origins of maize and the course of its development are matters of intense research and debate, for they touch upon important issues in genetics and anthropology and will provide keys to further improvement of the crop. Archaeological excavation has played an important part in this debate, furnishing dates and specimens of early maize, but it will be up to botanists and geneticists to provide a coherent description of the way that teosinte gave rise to primitive maize and how this, in turn, gave rise to later forms of maize. Progress has been made toward resolving some of the major enigmas of this history, but our understanding of the maize family tree remains far from complete.

One of the impediments to genetic analysis of the origins of maize is the lack of a stable base stock amenable to experimentation. Logically, one would study the key traits of maize against the genetic background of teosinte, since that would parallel the hypothetical direction of change, but while teosinte is available as a background stock, it has proved technically difficult to manipulate with molecular and morphological markers. As an alternative, a maize background would be acceptable if it could be made similar to the oldest Tehuacán maize, as I am attempting to accomplish.

At this point in maize research, the evidence seems to support the conclusion that at least two domestications of teosinte were involved in the origin of maize and that the genetic heritage of maize bred in the U.S. Corn Belt can be traced back to teosinte through two lines that I have termed the Southern Dent Pathway and the Northern Flint Pathway. These evolutionary lines began with different subspecies of teosinte that had different genetic tendencies to start with and that were then independently bred in different ways to solve the problem of freeing the teosinte seed (kernel) from its fruitcase, a tough, capsule-like enclosure individually protecting each seed. The two pathways are distinguishable not only on the basis of the cob characteristics created by these different ways of exposing the kernel but also in terms of kernel shape and growth habit.

According to my hypothesis, which I discuss in the 1991 edition of *Advances in Agronomy*, the Southern Dent Pathway originated from domestication of a teosinte subspecies commonly known as Chalco teosinte (*Zea mays* ssp. *mexicana*), which has a strong lateral branching tendency in comparison to other kinds of teosinte. Its breeding into primitive maize (now represented by the race Palomero Toluqueno in Mexico) entailed a reduction of the cupule, a cup-like part of the fruit-case. It shares both its lateral branching habit and this cob trait with a race of maize known as Pollo, found in Colombia, and another called Confite Morocho, which grows in the Andean highlands of Peru. All three plants are adapted for growth at intermediate to high altitudes, and presumably Pollo and Confite Morocho are relict forms of a primitive maize whose progenitor was Chalco teosinte. Advanced races of the Southern Dent Pathway also bear ears with many rows of kernels and tend to have kernels that are longer than they are wide.

In contrast, the Northern Flint Pathway is characterized by ears with only eight rows of kernels and by branching centered not in the lateral region along the stalk but rather at the base of the plant. This tendency for basal branching is inherent in maize derivatives stemming from domestication of a different teosinte subspecies (*Zea mays* ssp. *parviglumis*), first referred to as Balsas or Guerrero teosinte by its discoverer, H. Garrison Wilkes. Maizes of the Northern Flint Pathway also manifest their descent from Balsas teosinte in the fact that their kernels are wider than they are deep and have been exposed by being pushed out of the cupule through an elongation of the rachilla, which attaches each kernel to the cob at the base of the cupule.

In sum, in addition to their different branching habits, the Southern Dents and Northern Flints have opposite combinations of basic ear traits. Ears of the Southern Dent Pathway combine two evolved traits—many-rowed cobs and reduced cupules—with the primitive traits of kernels longer than they are wide and borne on short rachillae. Ears of the Northern Flint Pathway combine the evolved traits of wide kernels borne on elongate rachillae with the primitive characteristics of only eight rows borne in pairs with large cupules. The fact that these traits originating from teosinte linger in modern breeds of maize theoretically makes it possible to gauge the teosinte affinities of present, inbred lines and then to use this information to predict the outcome of crosses between them. Lines with different teosinte affinities should yield offspring with maximum hybrid vigor (heterosis).

History offers some support for this hypothesis, for when the Northern Flint and Southern Dent pathways converged and hybridized in the mid nineteenth century, the result was the world's most productive race of corn, the Corn Belt Dent, an outstanding example of hybrid vigor. In this case, the outcome should be attributed not only to the emergence of the two lines from different ancestral teosintes but also to the effects of their spread, isolation, and breeding into diverse geographical and ecological races of maize.

I reconstruct the history of this convergence as follows. The spread of maize north and northeastward from what is now the U.S. Southwest was delayed by environmental factors. The maize of this region and of adjoining areas of northern Mexico was adapted to long growing seasons, short days, and soil conditions ranging from arid to dry desert. As such, it was ill-adapted to move into the cooler, wetter lands to the north, but success was finally obtained with a large-kerneled derivative of the original eight-rowed type, a descendant of Balsas teosinte.

With this, the Northern Flint Pathway took shape. Starting about A.D. 700 in the Rio Grande valley, it spread northward on both sides of the Rocky Mountains. To the east, its route followed the major river valleys, whose floodplains were conducive to farming—the Arkansas, the Mississippi, the Platte, and the Ohio, among others. As maize continued northward and eastward into colder climates with wetter soils, shorter growing seasons, and longer days, there was selection—by natural forces or Indian growers, probably both—for larger and larger kernels that were wider than they were deep. Selection occurred as well for earlier flowering, a feature related to the basal branching trait inherent within this pathway. About A.D. 1200, maize of this type arrived in the area now thought of as upstate New York and New England, whose peoples found it an important supplement to food obtained by hunting, fishing, and gathering.

While archaeological evidence shows that eight-rowed maize was grown in the southeastern United States in pre-Columbian times, it probably stemmed from a branch (the Nal Tel branch) of the Northern Flint Pathway. The Southern Dent Pathway, with its many-rowed ears, has not been so fully traced but appears to have reached the southeastern corner of North America after A.D. 1500. I believe it was introduced by the Spanish, probably from stock they received in Cuba.

As already noted, the two pathways did not meet until the middle of the nineteenth century, when farmer settlers from the Northeast and the Southeast carried their respective races of maize out into the Midwest, setting off an inadvertent evolutionary explosion with great consequences for humankind. (Another factor contributing to this breakthrough was the steel plow, which made it possible to cultivate the thick sod of Midwestern prairies.) Because the Northern Flints tended to flower much earlier than the Southern Dents, the cross required late plantings of the Flint parent. To overcome this problem, the hybrid has since been inbred, with parental-like selections being used to replicate the hybrid vigor of the initial cross.

The legacy of the domestication and improvement of maize

has been advancement of civilizations throughout the world. Thanks to its tolerance for diverse soils and climates, maize has made productive land out of acreage that once had negligible agricultural use, expanding the food supply to support many more people than was previously possible. It is now one of the four principal food plants worldwide, the others being wheat, rice, and potatoes.

Continued increases in the productivity of maize and other crops, along with advances in agricultural technology, have now brought the United States to a point at which only about 4 percent of its people are engaged in agriculture, compared with 80 percent in 1800. Despite this huge reduction in the relative size of the farming population, the nation still grows enough maize to export a quarter of it—two billion bushels— to hungry parts of the world. According to figures published in 1990 by the U.S. Feed Grain Council, a little less than a third of this surplus goes to the Soviet Union, roughly a quarter is imported by Japan, and another quarter is divided among South Korea, Taiwan, and Mexico.

In the future, as population pressure and our understanding of maize both grow, this crop's role as our symbiotic partner in survival can only increase. As great as our power to adapt and improve food plants has been, the tool of molecular genetics should make it even greater in the future. The mingling of foods, technologies, and cultures from the Old World and the New affords the potential for everlasting human prosperity and peace—if only we can use our intelligence to improve our symbiotic relationship not only with plants but also with other people and, especially, with other nations.

CHAPTER 5

Beans of the Americas

LAWRENCE KAPLAN AND
LUCILLE N. KAPLAN

What is a bean, after all? The familiar English word comes from a root common to Old English, Old High German, and Old Norse that apparently once referred to the fava or faba bean, a staple of the Romans. Over the course of centuries the word has grown to encompass seeds of a multitude of legumes besides the fava, most of them belonging to other genera—a terminological tangle that botany avoids through the use of scientific names.

Fortunately, here we are concerned with the American beans, a more easily defined group since they all belong to a single genus, *Phaseolus*, of which just four species have been widely cultivated. Among the New World beans are many whose names, tastes, and uses are very well known—kidney, lima, pinto, wax, and navy beans—beans that have left their mark on the world at large. Other worthy American beans, however, including one entire species, remain undiscovered or unappreciated outside of specific regions or ethnic groups, and others, once better known, have slipped into relative obscurity.

From the writings of the sixteenth-century herbalists and from the later works of Linnaeus (1707–1778), the botanical genius who developed much of the scientific nomenclature for plants, and Augustin de Candolle (1778–1841), a great Swiss student of the origin of cultivated plants, it is clear that they did not know the geographic source of the common bean, *Phaseolus vulgaris*, the species most familiar and widespread today. The plant had found a place in European agriculture, and Linnaeus named it, but its past was a mystery until the last quarter of the nineteenth century, when archaeological excavations on the arid coast of Peru demonstrated that it had been cultivated there long before Columbus crossed the Atlantic.

Following that discovery, excavations elsewhere revealed the millennia-old American cultivation of the other three species as well: limas and sievas, scarlet runner beans, and teparies. Studying the beans' past has been simplified by the fact that, when archaeologists are fortunate enough to find ancient beans in desert sites or dry caves, the beans may be perfectly preserved—unable to germinate but fully recognizable by their colors and forms. From such discoveries, researchers have gained evidence of the geographic and botanical origin of the bean species and varieties, how long they have been cultivated, and what role they played in ancient subsistence and economy.

Varieties of the common bean were grown by Native Americans from as far south as Chile and Argentina to as far north as the St. Lawrence and upper Missouri River valleys. The earliest evidence for cultivation of the common bean comes from a cave in the Peruvian Andes, where seeds of fully domesticated varieties of this species have been found amid plant debris that yields radiocarbon dates as great as 8,000 years before the present. In the highland valley of Tehuacán, Mexico, deep cave deposits left by ancient peoples also contain many bean seeds, but the earliest evidence of beans there is a bit of common bean pod that has been estimated to be 6,000 or 7,000 years old and that is probably much more recent. Evidently the common beans came gradually northward from Mexico through Indian exchange, for in the southwestern United States the earliest remains of cultivated common beans located thus far were found in a New Mexico cave in a setting reckoned to be about 2,300 years old.

A second New World species, comprising the lima and sieva beans, has a somewhat more complicated past, both biologically and archaeologically. Linnaeus correctly recognized these beans as members of a single species, which he called *Phaseolus lunatus* to describe the "lunar" (half-moon) shape of the seeds of some varieties. The sieva types are small-seeded but will cross with the large-seeded limas and thus are considered to be of the same species. The two have very different histories of domestication, however.

Sievas appear in the archaeological records of Mexico about 1,200 years ago but do not turn up in the records of Andean archaeology. Limas, conversely, do not appear in the Mesoamerican or North American records but have been found in the same Andean cave as the earliest common beans, embedded in the same 8,000-year-old organic debris. This archaeological evidence of geographic separation coincides with contemporary observations of the distribution of both the wild and cultivated types of these beans. It seems clear that the two groups share a distant ancestor but long ago found different ecological niches and were domesticated independently by Andean and Mesoamerican native farmers.

In the northern coastal desert of Peru, well-preserved remains of lima varieties have been dated to 5,000 years ago and are so abundant that they must have constituted a major part of the diet. Ancient Peruvians even represented these beans in their imaginative painted ceramics and woven textiles, which gives us a reliable indication of the important part this food played in their subsistence. For instance, painted pottery from the Moche culture of A.D. 100–800 depicts running messengers, each carrying a small bag decorated with pictures of lima beans. Archaeologist Rafael Larco Hoyle has concluded that the lima beans—painted with parallel lines, broken lines, points, and circles—were ideograms, perhaps used in computation, but some images are certainly just renderings of naturally variegated seed coats. In other Moche artwork, stick-limbed lima bean warriors rush to the attack. Textiles from Paracas, an earlier coastal site, are also rich in bean imagery. It is noteworthy that the Moche examples, and probably all those from Paracas as well, represent lima beans. Limas appeared on the coast earlier than common beans and seem to have had greater social significance.

Specimens of the cultivated scarlet runner bean arrived in the Old World early enough for Linnaeus to know it and to name it *Phaseolus coccineus* for the brilliant color of its flowers. Pods of this bean that may be as much as 6,000 years old have been found in mountain caves in the state of Tamaulipas in northeastern Mexico, but botanists disagree on whether they were cultivated or were wild foods brought into the cave at that time. No cultivated forms of the bean are known in the archaeological record north of Durango, Mexico, where they were grown 1,300 years ago.

Both purple-seeded and white-seeded varieties of the runner bean have been grown by the Hopi in historic times and have been collected from them, especially by Alfred Whiting and his Hopi collaborators in the 1930s. The Hopi varieties closely resemble the long-known cultivars Scarlet Runner and White Dutch Runner, however, and are quite unlike the dark-colored native runner beans that predominate in the cool, southern Mexican highlands. This suggests that the beans came into Hopi hands by way of white missionaries or teachers rather than having migrated northward through pre-Columbian Indian exchange.

The tepary, *Phaseolus acutifolius*, is the only one of the cultivated New World species not to receive its scientific name from Linnaeus. The wild type was described and named by the nineteenth-century Harvard botanist Asa Gray, and not until the early years of the twentieth century were cultivated varieties recognized by Arizona botanist George F. Freeman as members of Gray's species rather than as varieties of the common bean. Still virtually unknown in commercial agriculture, teparies were first grown in central Mexico at a date yet to be verified and later, some 1,000 to 1,200 years ago, in Arizona.

Despite their antiquity and ancient distribution, teparies have been absent from village agriculture in historic times except in the Sonoran Desert of northwestern Mexico, Arizona, and New Mexico and in the area around Tapachula in the Mexican state of Chiapas and adjacent parts of Guatemala. Today they are grown and eaten by the Pima, the Papago, and peoples of the lower Colorado River and by some Anglo enthusiasts of crops adapted to dry lands. Because of their high drought tolerance, teparies have been tested with considerable success in many arid regions of the world.

Though archaeological data make it apparent that the four New World species of beans were all brought under cultivation in this hemisphere thousands of years ago, scholars can only begin to reconstruct the processes by which the beans were domesticated and dispersed. In the case of the common bean, for example, we know that the wild types grow as vines, and we can assume that the earliest domesticates were vining varieties, too. In the Americas, such vining or "pole" beans traditionally were planted with corn so that they could use the stalks for support, and this method remains in use in some areas.

Sprawling and dwarf varieties of the common bean, which may be grown independent of support, came into prominence long after the species was domesticated. Archaeological evidence indicates that bush or dwarf plants were grown in the Oaxaca Valley 1,000 years ago and in northeastern Mexico, in the state of Tamaulipas, 800 years ago. Exactly how this came to pass remains a matter of conjecture, but the Oaxaca and Puebla valleys of central Mexico were the scene of explosive population growth and the founding of permanent villages and urban centers in the interval between A.D. 100 and 700. By this time, agriculture was carried on in fields in which various forms of irrigation were devised to supplement seasonal rains. The expansion of agriculture into these drier lands would have favored bush beans, which have lower water needs than the older, vining types.

Later, as these areas were conquered by the Toltecs and Aztecs and were incorporated into their city-states, the exaction of tribute may have further affected agricultural practices, encouraging the production of crops such as bush beans that mature evenly and thus could be harvested all at once and reducing the production of vining beans, which mature irregularly and are picked over a long season. Such times of cultural change may be imagined to have fomented major changes in the relative production of different bean varieties.

In contrast with the prehistoric artistic renderings of beans in Peruvian textiles and ceramics, the imposing murals of the city-state of Teotihuacan, the great pre-Aztec center in the

Valley of Mexico, are richly ornamented with feathered serpents, flowering trees, maize, squash, and maguey but no beans—at least according to current interpretations. Yet beans are abundant at many archaeological sites in the Valley of Mexico and undoubtedly constituted part of the subsistence base of Teotihuacan's 100,000 to 150,000 residents. The Codex Mendoza, a post-Columbian Aztec pictorial document, depicts beans as objects in a game and, more important, as items of tribute delivered to the Aztec rulers. Beans, maize, cotton, textiles, garments, and other goods are all represented in the codex in such a way that the quantities exacted from each province of the Aztec empire can be estimated.

By the end of the fifteenth century, American beans had been shaped by the available genetic resources and by millennia of natural and human selection as well as by indigenous social developments. The arrival of the Spanish explorers and conquistadors ushered in a powerful new set of factors affecting bean stocks. Carl O. Sauer, the dean of American cultural geographers, pointed out long ago that as they explored, conquered, missionized, and settled New Spain, the conquistadors distributed both European and New World crop varieties. Through this great enterprise, they left an overlay of a newly introduced agriculture which took on the appearance of the indigenous.

For example, the black-seeded bush bean ubiquitous today in the highland Oaxaca Valley was present there, too, in pre-Columbian times but did not in any sense dominate the prehistoric array of beans. What happened, we believe, is that the Spanish conquest disrupted the native economy in a way that promoted the expansion of the black-seeded bean, resulting in regionwide use of a variety that had previously been restricted in locale.

Early contacts between Europeans and Native Americans,

starting with the second voyage of Columbus in 1493, began the outflow of beans from the well-established American production centers to Europe, Africa, the Mediterranean basin, and Asia. The American beans received their least enthusiastic welcome in Asia, where native legumes such as mung and adsuki "beans" were already grown in great variety. In some countries, India in particular, the flatulence occasioned by eating American beans created a second barrier to their acceptance.

On the other hand, American beans were readily accepted in the Iberian Peninsula, East Africa, Italy, central and eastern Europe, the Low Countries, and Britain. The great European herbals of the sixteenth century and those that appeared over the following two hundred years, all part of the publishing boom that followed the development of movable type, document the adoption and diversification of American bean stocks across Europe. As Old World farmers came into possession of the American legumes, they continued the process of selection and breeding that their New World counterparts had begun. Bringing to this task their own set of values and skills, they produced, in due course, dozens of new *Phaseolus* varieties.

Sixteenth- and seventeenth-century explorers and settlers mentioned finding "beans" and "pease" under cultivation in eastern North America, but presumably these names of Old World legumes were simply applied by analogy to New World species, with sieva types receiving the designation "beans" since they resemble the favas, and "pease" being used to indicate the smaller common bean. Judging from the lists of their shipboard supplies, the earliest British colonists did not bring any of the American beans back with them from England but rather adopted beans from the Native Americans who taught them to raise maize, beans, and squash. As the process of colonization continued, however, immigrants from agricultural or village backgrounds in continental Europe did carry their favored seed stocks to the New World, including varieties of *Phaseolus*. For instance, shell beans, a kind of common bean stripped from the pods when the seeds are mature but not yet dry, are said to have come to Pennsylvania by this means.

Other varieties of the common bean now traditional in the northeastern United States probably came directly from Peru, as did the large-seeded South American limas. The latter appear to have reached the United States in the early nineteenth century, for in his classic study, *Vegetables of New York*, U. P. Hedrick notes that in 1824 Captain John Harris of the U.S. Navy brought seed of this type from Lima and grew the plants on his farm at Chester, New York. By the late 1840s, lima beans were being shipped directly from Peru to California for consumption in the goldfields. It may be that at this time they received their now-customary name, a mispronunciation of Lima, their port of origin.

Many of the *Phaseolus* varieties brought to North America from Old World fields had been selected for succulent pods—that is, for use as snap beans rather than for the dry mature seeds—and this development shaped subsequent bean culture in the United States. Native Americans sometimes ate immature pods, as evidenced by the tangled remains of prehistoric pod fibers found at Mesa Verde in southwestern Colorado, but historical observations indicate that the main use of beans among Native Americans was as a mature, dry, storable seed crop. One economic historian who studied colonial-period documents of New England and letters of settlers who were captives of Indians in the seventeenth century has concluded that, as green vegetables, beans were unimportant to the Indians. F. W. Waugh, a Canadian ethnologist who described the foods of the early-twentieth-century Iroquois of Ontario, Quebec, and New York State, found that these Indian peoples classified no bean varieties as snap or string beans, although they did consume part of the pod along with cooked shell beans. In contrast to Native Americans and, in all likelihood, the early colonists, contemporary residents of the United States consume the common bean far more as a green vegetable than as a dried bean.

Historical records of bean diversity, production, and use may be helpful in piecing together North American bean culture, but they may also be frustrating. Information on crops of the colonial period, for example, may be culled from probate lists that were compiled for tax purposes upon the death of an estate owner. Since taxes could be paid in kind at the closing of the estate, officials inventoried holdings of wheat, maize, barley, and so on. Beans are absent from these lists, yet during the wars of the mid eighteenth century, records of the Massachusetts Bay Colony show that the government periodically banned exports of maize and beans from the port of Boston. In other words, on one hand, beans were not numbered among the crops of New England, but on the other, they were treated as an export commodity to be embargoed in times of peril.

Though archaeological retrievals and historical records furnish some idea of the uses and diversity of the American beans, one must turn to horticultural documents and to modern botany for a more complete picture. The common bean, for instance, is exceptionally diverse in terms of genetic variation—that is, the number of cultivars—included within the species. How can we determine how many cultivars such a species may comprise? One way to find out would be to go to a horticultural library—that at Cornell University's Bailey Hortorium, for example, or at the Massachusetts Horticultural Society—and to assemble all the seed catalogs for the past 150 years, list all the names, and count them. For *Phaseolus vulgaris*, this might net five hundred or even a thousand entries. The problem with this method is that a given cultivar might have several different names, which would result in some varieties being counted more than once. In addition, missing from the tally would be the cultivars not sold in catalogs, the "land races" grown by village folk for their own use.

In 1898, at the Missouri Botanical Garden in St. Louis, H. C. Irish undertook a large-scale study to overcome the shortcomings of such library research. Obtaining samples of all the varieties of common bean listed in the catalogs, he grew them in a single experimental garden in order to compare their characteristics. Likewise, over a period of years, horticulturists at Cornell University grew and compared a collection of beans that they described in a book titled *The Beans of New York*.

These two studies sought to mitigate systematic botany's pervasive and enduring problem of synonymy, the assigning of two or more names to a single cultivar. The resulting publications helped plant breeders of the day to understand the identity and heritage of the varieties with which they worked. For those who take interest today in preserving lesser-known varieties and even species of bean, it remains essential that continuous work be carried on to define varieties accurately. What is the advantage in acquiring bean seed that was grown for as long as anyone can remember by one family in a New Hampshire village if eventually it turns out to be genetically identical with Kentucky Wonder, an old catalog variety still very much available?

We confronted a dilemma of synonymy many years ago in the Oaxaca Valley, where the present-day market, as noted earlier, is overwhelmingly dominated by small-seeded black beans. These all grow on low, bushy plants, and most have one name in Zapotec and one in Spanish. Are they all one variety in the strict botanical sense? We spent a sabbatical year visiting village markets, talking to campesinos in their fields, and obtaining dozens of samples of these beans, then returned home and planted them in a university greenhouse to see if they all grew in the same way and had the same vegetative characteristics. Unfortunately, almost without exception the plants were so infected with growth-stunting viruses that their genetically controlled growth characteristics could not be discerned. With the hope that someday the stocks could be freed of viruses and grown again, we shelved the project. Besides, the sabbatical had come to an end. Somewhat later, with help from a biochemist colleague, we were able to test some of the seeds to determine differences in their protein enzymes and found some indication that there may be such differences.

In recent years, in the hands of Dr. Paul Gepts and others at the University of Wisconsin and the University of California at Davis, sophisticated analyses of protein structure have begun to produce solid data about synonymy among bean varieties and have greatly increased our knowledge of the geographic origins of groups of cultivars. Furthermore, comparative protein studies between cultivated varieties and wild beans collected by field botanists have revealed much about the geographic and temporal origins of the beans and about their diversity. Two of the four cultivated species, the common bean and the lima, prove to have had multiple geographic origins, and more data is emerging from the protein studies to show that, in general, multiple rather than single regions of origin are to be expected. It appears that distinct genetic populations of the common bean were domesticated independently in Mesoamerica, the Andes, and perhaps elsewhere in South America.

Despite the progress of bean research, problems of synonymy still plague efforts to track or even to estimate the losses of particular kinds of beans. It is safe to say, however, that a number of old American varieties have been lost, some of them even in this century. Anthropological studies of traditional foods provide much of the best data currently available, pinpointing disappearances of varieties from specific communities and locations. Though the losses documented in these studies often have been only local—with the varieties in question still grown elsewhere by other farmers—they suggest the rate at which heirloom bean stocks may be vanishing.

For instance, varieties of the small white baking and soup bean now produced in great abundance in Michigan were obtained from Indians of New York State sometime prior to the end of the nineteenth century, and by 1908 they were undergoing selection for disease resistance at Michigan Agricultural College. This small white bean is missing, however, from the sixty bean varieties that the ethnologist Waugh collected among the Iroquois between 1912 and 1915. Similarly, the sieva, or small-seeded lima bean, known to have been present in the Northeast at the time of the earliest contact between Europeans and Native Americans, was absent from Waugh's collection.

The loss of bean varieties may actually have accelerated in the past fifty years, driven by the forces of agglomeration operating in modern agriculture and merchandising. More and more, seeds available to home gardeners from glossy commercial catalogs are the same as those planted by agro-industry producers. Variations of Blue Lake, Romano, and Kentucky Wonder are typical catalog listings for pole beans, and the first two are the most commonly encountered in the frozen-food section of the local supermarket. King of the Garden and Fordhook are the universally offered limas, and the latter is among the most commonly grown commercial cultivars.

While market forces are now reducing bean diversity, in an earlier day they brought new varieties into being. A nineteenth-century effort to reduce the "stringiness" of snap beans, for example, is known to have been carried out by individual farmers, gardeners, and seed dealers and to have resulted in selections that differed significantly enough from their parental types to earn new cultivar names. In most cases, the names of the people who participated in such endeavors and the details of the process itself are lost, but in this instance they are preserved in the recollections of a veteran seedsman, Frank Taylor Woodruff.

Woodruff told a story of persistent selection over a long period to obtain the desired characteristics. In 1868 a produce wholesaler was approached by a Le Roy, New York, farmer who wanted to market bean seeds. The wholesaler, one Calvin N. Keeney, found a seedsman who agreed to market the seeds, and a number of other Le Roy farmers eventually joined in, entering the business of producing snap-bean seeds. Keeney recognized this as an opportunity to improve the varieties then being grown and set about developing a stringless, round-podded bean that would be easier to prepare for cooking and that would have a meatier pod wall.

Keeney took a variety called Refugee Wax as his starting point, since it had a rich yellow color, matured in midseason, and was round-podded. He gathered samples from the farmers of Le Roy and planted a large bed of the beans. As the pods reached cooking size, Keeney went from plant to plant, snapping beans to find the least stringy. Year after year he saved the mature seeds of the plants that had produced the least stringy pods. Offspring of this protracted selection process retained the stringless character and became known as Keeney's Stringless Refugee Wax, one of the first stringless snap beans.

Hybridizing by planting in such a way that bees could do the work of cross-pollination produced yet other new and popular bean varieties, including Burpee's Stringless Green Pod, the first known round and green-podded stringless bean, featured in that company's 1894 catalog. During the nineteenth century, seed producers in France, England, and Germany hybridized and selected garden beans as well, and though many of their new varieties were introduced into the United States, generally they did not prove successful. The reason: American growers had developed a pattern of picking their beans at a more mature stage than did the Europeans. Thus the European introductions tended to be tough or stringy by the time American farmers harvested them.

Breeding beans is one story, and eating all the new and old beans is another. At the onset of the Great Depression in 1930, U.S. census figures showed that household consumption of dry beans had a sharply negative correlation with income. In other words, the more affluent a family was, the fewer dry beans it ate. In fact, of twelve food groups on which data was collected, only the consumption of dry beans did not rise or remained roughly constant relative to income. Snap beans, though not specifically indexed, probably followed the more usual pattern, for the census found a positive correlation between high income and consumption of fresh vegetables.

Much the same pattern seems to hold today. Dry beans are scarcely a prestige food in the United States, frequently being associated with marginal subsistence. Nevertheless, they occupy a position peculiarly touched with nostalgia and in some cases offer a degree of regional and occupational identity. Boston is known as "the home of the bean and the cod." The old prospector in *The Treasure of the Sierra Madre* advises tenderfoot newcomers to "eat some beans" for strength on the trail. Navy beans, so hard of coat that they could be carried in sacks on shipboard without fear of sprouting if moisture got to them, still retain a trace of the romance of the open seas, and a logging camp may yet have its "bean hole," or cooking pot.

The nutritive value of beans is widely recognized but also widely misunderstood, owing to confusion regarding the chemical composition of foods as opposed to their dietary value. The human body utilizes bean protein less efficiently than it does protein from many other sources, so although dry beans or fresh shelled beans typically contain about 23 percent protein, much of their protein we cannot digest and assimilate. Nevertheless, beans are an excellent protein source, especially when the cost of bean protein is compared to that of animal protein. Also, utilization of bean protein can be improved by concurrent consumption of cereal grains or of the rich, highly digestible and assimilable proteins of eggs, dairy products, or animal flesh. In addition, dry beans are an excellent source of soluble and insoluble fiber.

Gassiness, long a subject of joke, rhyme, and embarrassment (the Renaissance herbalists did not fail to mention this trait), remains a problem for bean consumers. Some varieties seem to produce less gas than others, but much-touted gasless types have not lived up to their promise, at least not for everyone who has tried them. Suggestions for reducing gassiness, such as boiling the dried beans without first soaking them or soaking them overnight and pouring off the excess water, are subject to debate. One method that deserves more trial is also the most acceptable to bean lovers: consume beans regularly, daily. Some observe a decline in gassiness with regular consumption. If this doesn't work, eat beans anyway.

Throughout the world, beans have been used in the diet primarily as a nutritional complement to cereal grains and as a supplementary source of complex carbohydrates. Only in a few places is bean production sufficiently high to make them the principal calorie source. In Latin America, which many North Americans perceive to be a bean-rich environment, the *Phaseolus* beans actually play a modest role in rural economies and diets since their yields are relatively low (for the amount of labor expended and land occupied) compared with starchy crops such as maize, wheat, potatoes, manioc, and plantains. Thus, ironically, beans are at the same time a food of the poor in rich societies and a food that the poor in poor societies may be able to afford only in small quantities.

The fate of bean varieties in the United States is hard to predict. The Scarlet Runner, which we personally have championed as one of America's most neglected garden vegetables, clearly is more neglected than ever. U.S. catalogs now rarely carry this lovely bean at all or, if they do, list just one cultivar. British catalogs, on the other hand, offer as many as seven types, varying in height, earliness, color of flowers and seeds, and other characteristics. When grown in regions of long and not-too-hot summers such as the Pacific Northwest and New England, the Scarlet Runner produces what those who know them regard as the best-flavored of all green beans. Some gardeners grow them purely as ornamentals for their exuberant vines and red, red-white, or white flowers.

In the U.S. Southwest, most of the bean varieties found in the ancient caves are no longer available in cities and towns, but the tireless work of Gary Nabhan and others has led to the recovery of some of these varieties, and through such non-profit groups as the Seed Savers Exchange and Native Seeds/ SEARCH, these are again available to the thoughtful and adventurous gardener. One restored to availability is the Jacob's

Cattle bean, which was in the Southwest in prehistoric times and which mysteriously became a traditional bean of New England. The Jacob's Cattle type is not found among prehistoric beans of the Midwest, Ohio, or New York State, yet it reached Maine and northern New England in the historic period. There is still a bit of wonder in beans.

John Withee of Lynnfield, Massachusetts, deserves credit for helping to lay the foundation for contemporary efforts at bean preservation. A medical photographer by trade, for decades he was also an indefatigable collector, grower, and disseminator of heritage bean varieties. Until the early 1980s, Withee exchanged noncommercial bean seeds with his network of correspondents and distributed them to others who subscribed to his newsletter and catalog, which carefully noted cases of synonymy. The Seed Savers Exchange now lists his and many other heritage varieties in its *Garden Seed Inventory*, with *Phaseolus* beans running to forty-three pages in the second edition.

When a contemporary columnist wrote not long ago of pulling and stacking bush Red Kidney beans during his boyhood on a New Hampshire farm, he recalled the pride that farmers took in bean varieties that had come down through the decades: Jacob's Cattle, Soldier, Bonnemain, China Red Eye, Golden Eyed, Coach Dog, Speckled Beauty, Hidatse Red, Ground Bird, Turtle, Dwarf Wren's Egg. Six of these old New Hampshire cultivars, or closely related types, are currently offered by the Vermont Bean Seed Company, the commercial U.S. source that today offers the largest inventory of bean varieties. Its catalog also lists a number of other traditional cultivars and some recent introductions adapted to the Northeast. Here, too, are lima beans of both Mesoamerican and Andean types and white- and purple-seeded runner beans. Indeed, the catalog contains beans in every principal category of growth and use: yellow- and green-podded, even a type whose green is obscured by purple; pole and bush beans; snap beans; shell beans; and those used as dry, mature seeds.

Thankfully, those who work for the preservation of bean varieties are motivated in part by preservation as a goal in itself. But in preservation there is also the security of knowing that a variety that is merely interesting today may tomorrow fill a special requirement in food production for the human diet.

Try some of these lesser-known varieties of beans. They are often challenging to grow, and if you can't eat all you harvest or if you harvest only a few, you can use them to send messages or play games.

The Peripatetic Chili Pepper: Diffusion of the Domesticated Capsicums Since Columbus

JEAN ANDREWS

Ic is the New World chili pepper that gives the characteristic bite to many Old World cuisines. What would the food of India be without curry—or curry powder without peppers? Indonesia's sambals without their distinctive fire? Hungary's goulash without paprika? Italy's antipasto without pepperoni? Five hundred years ago, none of the people in these countries had ever seen or heard of a chili pepper. No Old World language had a word for chili peppers before 1492.

For Christopher Columbus, reaching the New World constituted a failure to achieve his objective, which was to find a route to the spice lands of the Far East, and he died thinking that he had found the fabled Orient instead of the New World with its vastly different kinds of riches. One of these treasures was the pungent flavoring widely used in the Americas and, on the islands of the Caribbean, referred to as *aji*. Columbus called the unfamiliar spice "pepper" (*pimiento*) after the black pepper (*pimienta*) he was seeking.

Columbus carried specimens of the new pepper, which belongs to the genus *Capsicum*, back to the Iberian Peninsula, and from there it spread rapidly around the globe, changing and enhancing the cuisines of every land it touched. Today it may be the most widely used spice in the world. Certainly it ranks high on the list, alongside black pepper (*Piper nigrum*), which is derived from an unrelated plant.

So swiftly and thoroughly did the chili pepper disperse that botanists long held it to be native to India or Indochina, but all scholars now concur that it is a New World plant with origins in South America. Researchers still disagree, however, about just where the capsicums arose. One group, led by W. Hardy Eshbaugh, says its place of origin was central Bolivia, while another, whose chief proponent is Barbara Pickersgill, claims that it was the area east of Bolivia in the mountains of southern Brazil. It seems safe to say that chili peppers originated in the area south of the wet forests of Amazonia and the semiarid cerrado of Brazil.

The prehistoric migration of wild capsicums from this area occurred thanks to birds, humans, or both. (It is difficult to differentiate between the roles of these two agents.) The pungent red fruits of wild chili peppers such as the Chiltepín are erect, easily separated from the stalk when ripe, and small enough for birds to swallow. The ingested seed may be carried a considerable distance before it is dropped, whereupon it often quickly establishes itself. Humans, too, could have carried and even cultivated wild peppers without changing them genetically, beginning any time after the formation of the Panama land bridge between North and South America in the Pleistocene epoch.

By the time Europeans arrived in the New World, peppers had migrated from South America into Mesoamerica and the Caribbean, and all five of the domesticated forms that we now recognize had been developed. *Capsicum annuum* var. *annuum*, domesticated in Mesoamerica (probably in Mexico), has become the most economically important variety, giving us Cayenne and Bell peppers as well as Jalapeños. *Capsicum frutescens*, first cultivated in the western Amazon basin, has given us another of the best-known peppers, Tabasco. *Capsicum chinense* also appears to have been domesticated in western Amazonia, and some scholars, including Charles B. Heiser, Jr., and A. T. Hunziker, suggest that it should properly be grouped with *Capsicum frutescens* as a single species. Only these three forms were found outside of South America before the arrival of Columbus, and they alone have become established in the Old World.

The remaining two forms, *Capsicum baccatum* var. *pendulum* and *Capsicum pubescens*, were both brought under cultivation in South America, and the former is still found only there. *Capsicum pubescens* migrated north to Central America and Mexico perhaps as late as this century, although Pickersgill believes it came northward with the conquistadors by the middle of the sixteenth century. Neither of these peppers is well known to North American consumers.

Since the time of Western contact, it has definitely been we humans who have promoted the diffusion of chili peppers. While wild peppers can be spread by human or other means, such domesticated varieties as Bell and Jalapeño peppers have been so altered that they can only be spread by human activity, and during the first century of the post-Columbian period, human intervention on a grand scale resulted in worldwide introduction of the three peppers now best known. Many of their domesticated forms had small fruits that dried well, making them easy to transport, and had seed that remained viable for long periods. The fact that chili pepper was the most common spice used by the Native Americans, combined with its ease of transportation, virtually assured it a place on early voyages back to Spain.

Heiser and Pickersgill both believe that the first peppers Columbus and his men encountered were probably *Capsicum chinense* and *Capsicum frutescens*. Another candidate, put forth by Hardy Eshbaugh, is the undomesticated *Capsicum annuum*. On his last voyage (1502–1504), Columbus very likely came across *Capsicum annuum* var. *annuum* during his visits to the Mayan coast of present-day Honduras. In 1519, when the conquistadors invaded Mesoamerica, they not only found this most economically important of the capsicums but also learned its Nahuatl name, *chilli*. The Spaniards converted the word to *chile* and the English to *chili*, and chili peppers we have had ever since.

Portuguese voyagers to Brazil encountered the same three types of chili pepper that the Spaniards found in Meso-america. Pickersgill reports that *Capsicum baccatum* var. *pendulum* grew in Brazil at the time of the Portuguese conquest, but I have found no evidence that they introduced it to the Old World. As for *Capsicum pubescens*, it is difficult to grow except in high elevations like those of its Andean homeland, and its fruit does not dry satisfactorily, so even if the Portu-guese encountered it, it probably would not have traveled well outside South America.

The introduction of domesticated peppers to a few Old World countries has been clearly documented, but in other cases the dates and avenues of the peppers' introduction can, at this point, only be deduced from indirect data. One impor-tant key to reconstructing the post-Columbian distribution of capsicums and other New World plants is the papal Treaty of Tordesillas, which dates from 1494 and which effectively divided the globe into Spanish and Portuguese spheres of influence. The treaty, often overlooked by botanists, drew a longitudinal line 370 leagues west of the Cape Verde Islands, giving Spain the right to explore and trade in the area to the west while reserving the eastern half of the globe for Portugal, including the route around southern Africa to Asia. In the Far East, the boundary was only vaguely located, so in 1529 the conflicting claims were settled by the Treaty of Zaragosa, which awarded Spain control of the Philippines and gave Portugal all rights to the Spice Islands.

In 1580, about fifty years after this Far Eastern dispute was negotiated, the two great Iberian powers were united under a single king, Henry II, but each country remained autonomous in its overseas colonial empire. Not until the end of the sixteenth century, when Dutch ships reached the Strait of Malacca, did any other European nation succeed in diminishing Iberian power in the Far East. By that time, capsicums and other American plants had spread throughout the region and beyond, reaching all but Australia and the islands of Polynesia.

The Portuguese part of this saga of exploration and trade began more than half a century before Columbus reached the Americas. Under the guidance of Prince Henry the Navigator, the Portuguese began their imperial quest on the western coast of Africa, and by 1460 they had traversed the bulge extending from Cape Bojador to Cape Verde and Sierra Leone. They continued down the coast, bit by bit, until in 1488 Bartholomeu Dias rounded the Cape of Good Hope and sighted the Indian Ocean.

During these years the Portuguese began trading in slaves and African goods while continuing their search for spices, gold, and additional sources of slaves. Six years after the discovery of America, Vasco da Gama arrived in India via the Cape of Good Hope and the Indian Ocean, thereby establishing the Portuguese trade monopoly earlier guaranteed by the

Treaty of Tordesillas. During the following century of unchallenged dominion, Portuguese vessels transported New World plants and goods, including chili peppers, along this route to Africa and the Far East.

After 1493, peppers from the Spanish Main were available to the Portuguese for trade in their western African colonies, and in the first decades of the next century, Brazilian chili peppers also became available as the Portuguese themselves explored and colonized Pernambuco in easternmost Brazil, the only part of the New World that lay on the Portuguese side of the papal boundary. Africans liberally used their native "Grains of Paradise," or melequeta peppers (*Aframomum melequeta*, a ginger unrelated to either the black pepper or the chili pepper), in their spicy cooking, so they were quick to adopt the new American peppers, and capsicums were disseminated virtually throughout Africa, as far as Mozambique on the southeastern coast.

The breadth of the chili peppers' dispersion in Africa resulted in part from a Portuguese policy intended to prevent unity among slaves and thus to reduce the likelihood of rebellion. This policy, which prohibited plantations from having large concentrations of slaves from a single geographic area, stimulated a far-reaching search for new sources of slaves, and where the slave traders went, chili peppers evidently soon followed. By the time the British came to dominate the slave trade a century and a half later, American peppers had become so important to Africans that their British captors included them among the staples on their slave vessels. Through these means, three of the American peppers—*Capsicum frutescens, Capsicum chinense*, and *Capsicum annuum* var. *annuum*—came to be grown in Africa.

Portuguese traders introduced the capsicums to India with equal speed, and three varieties of chili peppers were seen there by 1542. According to the early European botanist Carolus Clusius, *Capsicum* was known in Goa by the middle of the sixteenth century as "Pernambuco pepper." Apparently, Brazilian chili peppers were loaded aboard ships bound for Lisbon, where they were transferred to the huge carracks of the India fleet that annually made the long voyage around Africa to Goa, and some of the peppers carried with them to the Malabar Coast the name of their supposed place of origin in Brazil.

Like Arabic, Chinese, Persian, Hebrew, Greek, and Old Latin, Sanskrit has no ancient name for capsicums, and today very hot pickles are widely known in India as *achaar*, a word derived in part from *ají*. Hot peppers themselves are called *chillies*, from the original Nahuatl name. The American peppers were swiftly accepted in spice-loving tropical India and were soon cultivated there for export to other regions of Asia, as well as to the Middle East and Europe. The exact identity of the early introductions has not been determined, but *Capsicum annuum* var. *annuum* of the Cayenne type presently dominates the region.

New World capsicums reached the East Indies (Indonesia) by 1540, according to Henry N. Ridley. They were introduced either by the Portuguese or by Arab and Gujarati traders, who had been active in Southeast Asia for a thousand years. Since 1511, Malacca had served as a forward base for Portuguese trading and missionary expansion into China (1513), Japan (1542), and eastern Melanesia, and by 1550 the Portuguese had a permanent foothold on Macao. Their trading galleon, the *Nao da Macao*, ran from Goa via Malacca to Macao and thence to Nagasaki, Japan, until the mid seventeenth century. From any of these Portuguese ports of call, local seagoing craft—Malaccan, Javanese, Siamese (Thai), Cambodian, and Chinese, as well as Indian and Arabic—could easily have carried American peppers throughout the East Indies and the Spice Islands (the Moluccas) and even to the Philippines and China. The chili peppers may also have been disseminated by traders with Arab and Persian colonies that had been established during the seventh and eighth centuries in Canton and Hangchow, on China's southeast coast.

In any case, capsicums soon spread in cultivation throughout the area and then escaped from gardens to naturalize in the wild. Birds again are suspected of having played an important role in seeding the peppers in remote places, but according to Ridley the chili peppers "do not appear to have occurred in oceanic islands until brought by man." Ridley suggests that dried or fresh chili peppers were taken as a condiment or food by Malay, Indian, and other sailors, thus spreading into the far reaches of the Pacific. He also notes that when capsicums ripen in the islands of New Caledonia, flocks of pigeons descend from the mountains to feed on them. Though some Pacific islands were inaccessible to humans, few are so remote that chili pepper seeds could not have been deposited there by birds.

Although the introduction of chili peppers to China is not documented, like other American crops they took root in Chinese soil before 1550, even within the lifetime of the conquistadors. Alfred Crosby observes in *The Columbian Exchange* that "no large group of the human race in the Old World was quicker to adopt American food plants than the Chinese," and American peppers may have reached them by several means. Trade and pilgrimage routes between China and India and between China and the Moslem Middle East are known to have been avenues of penetration for some American plants and are the most likely routes for the capsicums. Pungent dishes served in American Chinese restaurants attest to the fact that Chinese pepper culture and use attain their height in cuisine of the Yunnan and Szechuan provinces, which are crossed by an ancient silk road that linked India and China even before the time of Christ.

It is probable, however, that the new spice also reached China by one or more sea routes. In their southern ports the Chinese maintained intimate trade relations with the Portuguese, particularly after the founding of the Portuguese trading colony in Macao. Chinese merchants also dealt with the Portuguese in the Spice Islands and with the Spanish in the Philippines, and either of these places may have served as their source of the hot little fruits from America. During that early period there was no regular overland trade to carry capsicums between the coastal cities and interior provinces like Yunnan or Szechuan.

The Portuguese reached Japan in 1549, and from then until 1636, when Japan closed its doors to all except the Dutch, there was ample time for the trading galleon from Goa to bring Japan its first capsicums. On the other hand, the Japanese may have come in contact with chili peppers through trading missions of their own, as Japanese vessels were already plying the waters of Southeast Asia by the time the Portuguese arrived in Japan. Using ships built from Spanish designs, the Japanese also had some direct trade with the west coast of New Spain, in what is now Mexico, until access was denied in 1611.

Portugal put the Philippines on European maps in 1512, but it was Spain that colonized the archipelago after Ferdinand Magellan claimed it for Spain in 1521. The first settlers were sent out from New Spain in 1542, and the first capsicums may have come with them. In 1564, after the Spanish navigator Andrés de Urdaneta showed that it was possible to sail to Mexico from the Far East by following prevailing westerlies, a Manila–Acapulco galleon route was established, providing regular contacts between the two ports for the next two and a half centuries and thus expediting the introduction of American food plants not only to the Philippines but also to Micronesia and eastern Melanesia. To this day, Filipinos refer to many of these plants by names adapted from Native American languages.

As a result of the Treaty of Tordesillas, during the sixteenth century the Spanish enjoyed virtually unrivaled mastery in the Pacific Ocean. They controlled not only the Philippines but also Micronesia and eastern Melanesia until they ceded the latter to the Portuguese in 1529. This act gave the Portuguese dominion throughout Melanesia as well as ports in China and Japan, and their regime was not broken until other European nations ventured into the region at the beginning of the seventeenth century. By that time, American food plants, including capsicums, had become well established.

Curiously, Europe itself proved to be slow when it came to accepting the New World peppers. In an epistle dated 1493, Peter Martyr wrote that Columbus had brought Spain "pepper more pungent than that from the Caucasus," and although we are told by Oviedo (1526) that in the New World "Christians"—meaning the Spanish colonists—were quick to eat the new spice in as great a quantity as the natives did, stay-at-home Spaniards seem to have been less culinarily adventurous. We can safely assume that chili peppers were being grown on the Iberian Peninsula as early as 1493, but they were favored more as curiosities and ornamentals than as seasoning. Unlike their creole and mestizo relations in the New World, Iberians even today have not acquired a taste for the fiery fruit.

Chili peppers reached the rest of Europe by two different pathways. Of the two, the more direct was transport by Iberian vessels from Lisbon and Seville, which carried the capsicums to Antwerp and other ports in western Europe.

Presumably it was by this means that the peppers arrived in England by 1548, for the British were not yet active in either the West or East Indies at that date. English traders probably acquired the seed either from Spain or from nearby Antwerp, where a Portuguese mercantile colony was then flourishing.

The American peppers traveled a far more circuitous route to the eastern Mediterranean and to central and eastern Europe: they were obtained by Moslem merchants in India (which the Portuguese lumped together with East Africa), and were then shipped via the Persian Gulf or the Red Sea to Aleppo, Alexandria, or both, and from there were transported northward. Details of the peppers' passage from India have not yet been discovered, but two theories seem most likely to be substantiated. One holds that merchants trading with Europe obtained capsicums from Portuguese colonies on the Malabar and Swahili coasts as they traveled the ancient trade routes along the Persian Gulf to India. In 1570 the Flemish botanist Matthias de Lobel observed that the Portuguese had introduced capsicums into Goa at a very early date and possibly began exporting them in competition with black pepper. Since Ormuz (Hormuz) was a Portuguese colony and spice trading center from 1515 to 1662, there is a strong possibility that chili peppers found their way to eastern Europe through this port.

More likely, the influx of chili peppers from Asia was of Turkish origin. It is unknown where the Turks got them, but it would have been easy for the Turkish armies to carry peppers as they traveled along the medieval trade routes through the Persian Gulf, across Asia Minor to the Black Sea, and on into Hungary, which they had conquered in 1526. Seeds passing along this route reached Germany before 1542, when the Bavarian physician and botanist Leonhart Fuchs published an herbal containing a description of four peppers. Believing that the German stock had come from India, Fuchs called the spice "Calicut pepper" and "Indian pepper."

In any case, the American peppers' round-about path to central and eastern Europe created many decades of confusion. Even though the eighteenth-century botanists Georg Rumpf, Carolus Linnaeus, and Phillip Miller all listed America as chili peppers' place of origin, Europeans in general believed they came from India until 1868, when Augustin de Candolle published a comprehensive treatise advancing linguistic and other reasons to recognize the New World as the capsicums' first home.

Like the Portuguese and Spanish, other western Europeans were slow to take to chili peppers. Eastern Europeans integrated them more readily into local food patterns, but Europeans as a whole did not widely appreciate their value as a spice until the first decade of the nineteenth century, when capsicums were reintroduced from the Balkans during the Napoleonic blockade of European ports and won acceptance as a substitute for other imported seasonings.

Ironically, the capsicums came very late to North America. Except for the two Spanish colonies of Santa Fe and Saint Augustine, chili peppers were to be found nowhere north of modern-day Mexico until after colonization by northern Europeans. About 1600 the Dutch, English, and French broke the Iberian trade monopoly in the Far East, and the spice market became a free-for-all. Thus, both the British and the Dutch had ample sources of peppers by the time they began to colonize North America early in the seventeenth century, but peppers did not take hold there until later, when the plantation system and African slavery were instituted. Southern plantations had a climate suitable to the cultivation of peppers, and the African slaves, both from the West Indies and directly from Africa, had already developed eating patterns that demanded hot peppers.

Thus capsicums traveled from the New World to the Old and back again to Europe by way of the Orient—all before the arrival of the Pilgrims at Plymouth Rock. During the time required for that journey, peoples of Africa, India, the Middle East, and the Far East so completely incorporated the new spices into their cookery that each area had developed not only a unique cuisine based on capsicums but also unique peppers not to be found in the Americas today.

The five original domesticated forms have given rise to hundreds of varieties of capsicums worldwide. This is many more, of course, than any grocer could stock, but thanks to the rising ethnic diversity in the United States and the increasing appreciation of Mexican, Indonesian, Thai, Vietnamese, and other non-European cuisines, a broader selection of capsicums has begun to appear in supermarket produce displays. Sadly, most U.S. residents continue to restrict their fresh pepper purchases to the bland, indigestible green Bell pepper.

Perhaps native-born North Americans are handicapped by a late start when it comes to eating peppers, but some of us are making up for lost time. I admit that I am addicted to these zesty little fruits, and I have instructed the mockingbirds that feast on the peppers in my Texas garden to deposit seeds on my grave so that I will never run out.

CHAPTER 7

Forgotten Roots of the Incas

NOEL VIETMEYER

Along the length of western South America, Inca towns and villages dot the Andes like flecks of color in a great, wrinkled cape. The farmers who tilled these mountainsides at the time of the Inca empire, about five hundred years ago, were among the best of the ancient world, and some would argue that their descendants are today the world's foremost practitioners of organic agriculture.

On slopes rising four vertical miles up the spine of the whole continent, in climates varying from tropical to polar, the Incas cultivated almost as many species of plants as the farmers of all of Asia. Without money, iron, written language, or the wheel, in the fifteenth century the Incas terraced and irrigated these precipitous heights to produce abundant food for fifteen million or more subjects. Throughout a vast territory that sprawled from southern Colombia to central Chile—an extent as great as that of the Roman Empire, which at its zenith stretched from Britain to Persia—their storehouses overflowed with grains, root crops, and dried meats.

In 1531, when Francisco Pizarro and the conquistadors invaded Peru, they initiated events that would elevate one obscure Inca crop to a high place in Western gastronomic culture. The potato, an Inca staple previously unknown outside the Andes, proved a convenient food for sailors on the treasure galleons, and thus it was carried, almost inadvertently, to Europe. In the four and a half centuries since the conquest, the potato has become one of the twenty essential crops that feed humanity.

But Pizarro and the adventurers who conquered Peru came seeking gold, silver, and religious converts, not plants. They considered the Incas backward and uncreative, and as a result of their rule, much of the intricate, marvelously productive agricultural system fell into ruin. Some Andean crops that had occupied honored positions in Inca society virtually disappeared. Others were all but abandoned in favor of European crops such as wheat and barley, which the conquerors demanded.

Today in the high Andes, however, vestiges of the Inca past remain, as rural peasants continue to grow the crops of their illustrious forebears. In local markets, Quechua women with parched, leathery features and wearing derby hats and crimson jackets display piles of roots, grains, and fruits, almost all of which are still foreign to visitors from North America or the Old World.

Among them are at least five species of cultivated potatoes that the Spanish left behind. Peruvian Indians actually have about two hundred names for the many kinds of potatoes found in the Andes, a group that includes more than a hundred species of wild potatoes. Collectively, these species are adapted to a wide array of climates and constitute a giant repository of biological diversity and disease resistance. Only recently have they begun to receive agronomic recognition.

Many of these little-known potatoes have unusual properties. A number are bitter tasting but turn sweet after being
frozen and dried to make a food the natives call *chuño*. Some
of the Andean potatoes are completely black inside, others
golden yellow. Some can withstand the severest cold, dozens
have notable flavors (a decidedly nutty taste, for instance), and
almost all are more nutritious than the particular white potato
species that the rest of the world relies on.

In the main, these "other potatoes" produce small tubers—
not surprising, given the lack of commercial research attention
they have received—but their immediate economic potential
is apparent. British agronomist R. W. Gibson has found, for
example, two species of Bolivian wild potato whose leaves
are veritable minefields to insects. Alighting on one of these
plants, even a minute aphid—one of the potato farmer's major
enemies—breaks open tiny, four-lobed hairs that blanket the
surface of the leaves, releasing a sticky goo that adheres so
firmly to the insect's legs that it becomes stuck to the leaf
and dies. This gluelike substance is strong enough to catch a
leafhopper by the jaws when it tries to bite into a leaf. While
these particular wild potatoes are themselves unsuitable as
food crops, researchers are beginning to breed them with the
common potato to give it such pest-trapping hairs. Other
cultivated and wild Andean potatoes are receiving research
recognition as well, notably from the International Potato
Center in Lima, Peru, but generally they remain little known
in potato-growing areas and potato-research facilities around
the world.

Even setting aside all these types of potatoes, the Incas domesticated and grew more root crops than any other culture
on Earth. Their fields produced at least nine other tuber crops
from botanical families as diverse as mustard, legume, and
sunflower. As if to emphasize this abundance, each of these

tubers itself appears in a myriad of colors, shapes, and sizes. No doubt, like other native peoples, the Incas intentionally selected for and preserved some of these unusual features, especially color.

Consider oca (*Oxalis tuberosa*), for example. An exceptionally hardy plant that above ground looks somewhat like clover, oca produces a profusion of wrinkled tubers in an array of shapes and sizes and in almost all the colors of the rainbow: red, orange, yellow, violet, purple, and white. In the Andean highlands, it ranks second only to the potatoes in its importance among the root crops and is a staple of Peruvian and Bolivian Indians living at altitudes up to about 13,500 feet.

Although so far it is almost unknown to the rest of the world, oca has become popular in New Zealand in the last twenty years and is now marketed (under the misleading name "yam") throughout the country. New Zealanders serve it on special occasions—boiled, baked, or fried—instead of the commonplace potato. Its firm white flesh has a high sugar content, and its pleasant, slightly sour taste has won it a reputation as "the potato that doesn't require sour cream."

Oca got to New Zealand via an English immigrant who picked up some tubers in Chile in the 1860s. Since then it has been grown sporadically as a minor backyard vegetable and ornamental. The plant is suitably adapted for the conditions found throughout New Zealand's North Island and is producing commercial yields that average three to four tons per acre. Since the climate and latitude of New Zealand are similar to those of agricultural regions in North America and Europe, oca certainly possesses the potential to become a common vegetable in Western cuisine during the next twenty years. It also holds promise for the highlands of Asia and Africa and should be tested there.

Arracacha (*Arracacia xanthorrhiza*) is another Inca root

with the potential to make a contribution around the world. The late David Fairchild, dean of U.S. plant explorers prior to World War II, considered it "much superior to carrots," and thousands of inhabitants of the Andes agree with him. In many areas of the mountains, arracacha replaces the potato since it costs only half as much to plant and harvest.

Arracacha was so completely overlooked in colonial times that it was not even given a scientific name until three hundred years after the Spanish conquest. Above ground the plant somewhat resembles celery, to which it is related, while below ground it produces crunchy, smooth-skinned roots similar to carrots but with white, yellow, or purple flesh. Added to stews or eaten boiled or fried as a table vegetable, arracacha roots have a delicate flavor that combines the savors of celery, cabbage, and roasted chestnut.

Arracacha is still almost as little known scientifically as it was at the time of Columbus, but it is eaten in most Latin American countries as far north as Costa Rica and reportedly is also found in Cuba and Haiti. Arracacha roots are sold in considerable quantities in the larger cities of Colombia, and recently they have gained popularity in such urban centers of southern Brazil as São Paulo, where they are called *mandioquinha-salsa*. Already a Swiss-based company uses arracacha to season a dried soup that is widely sold in Brazil, suggesting that people outside Latin America may also soon be enjoying this long-overlooked root.

Prospects for maca (*Lepidium meyenii*), a turnip-like plant in the mustard family, are not so bright. Steven King, a botanist specializing in Latin American plants and one of the few to have studied this crop, estimates that only twenty-five acres of it remain, all of them in the stark environs and bone-chilling climate around Lake Junin in Peru. This region is so high and harsh that only one other crop, bitter potatoes, can survive.

Indeed, at its highest point—14,000 feet—maca is being cultivated at a greater altitude than perhaps any other crop on Earth; without it, agriculture there would be impossible.

A relative of cress, the European salad vegetable, maca is a matlike perennial so small that even visiting botanists have been known not to realize when they were standing in a farmer's field. Its tiny leaves are edible and have traditionally been eaten in salads or used to fatten guinea pigs for the table. The bulbous roots, which look like brown radishes, are rich in sugar and starch and have a distinctly sweet, tangy flavor that has made them a delicacy in the high Andean plateau region of Peru and Bolivia. Maca roots are usually roasted or boiled in milk or water to form a sort of gruel, but they may also be dried, which makes them soft and chewy and allows them to be stored for years. Maca's nutritional content is unknown, as is its viability as a crop in other locales, and unless something is done to protect this fine food, these questions will soon be moot.

Ahipa (*Pachyrrhizus ahipa*) is a climbing vine that grows rapidly and produces remarkable yields. It is a legume, but unlike its relatives the pea, bean, and peanut, it develops swollen, fleshy roots weighing as much as ten pounds each. These succulent white tubers have a pleasant, sweet taste akin to water chestnut and are as crisp as apples. Ahipa (pronounced a-*hee*-pa) is often sliced thin and eaten raw in green salads and fruit salads. It is also sometimes lightly steamed or boiled and has the unusual property of retaining its crunchiness even after cooking.

Though essentially unknown outside the South American continent, ahipa has won favor in some islands of the West Indies, where British scientists from Kew Gardens introduced it during the nineteenth century. A closely related tuber, perhaps even a member of the same species, is the jicama, which is much-loved in its Central American homeland and in the Philippines (where its name has been modified to *sinkamas*) and is becoming popular in the United States as a low-calorie snack food and salad ingredient. Ahipa could meet with the same enthusiasm. While sharing jicama's refreshing quality, as a member of the legume family it has an advantage over all competitors: rhizobia bacteria in its root nodules make nitrogenous compounds available to the plant, thus enabling it to flourish even in poor soils and enriching the earth as it grows.

Another root sometimes compared (and confused) with jicama is yacon (*Polymnia sonchifolia*), a distant relative of the sunflower. Cultivated in temperate valleys from Colombia to northwest Argentina, sometimes at elevations as high as 10,000 feet, it produces tubers resembling those of the garden dahlia. Fused together, they splay out like fat spokes from a hub, and a single bunch can weigh as much as five pounds.

Yacon tubers are earth-colored on the outside, white on the inside, and have the consistency of a turnip. Eaten raw, their sweetish, succulent character makes them a rival to jicama and ahipa, and like ahipa they may also be cooked. Yacon's main stem is sometimes used as a celery-like vegetable, and the plant shows promise as an animal fodder as well as for human consumption.

This ancient crop of the tropical and subtropical Andes is today most often found in small, family plots, not in markets. Before World War II it was introduced to Italy and elsewhere in southern Europe, where it was studied as a possible source of sugar and forage, but the war interrupted this work, and yacon has not become established there. Nonetheless, the fact that it grew successfully in that temperate, lowland region at a much higher latitude than its native area shows that yacon could have worldwide potential like the potato.

Probably the most striking root in Andean markets is the ulluco (*Ullucos tuberosus*), whose tubers are so flamboyantly colored—yellow, pink, red, even candy-striped—and so shiny that visitors might mistake them for plastic. Ulluco (pronounced oo-*yoo*-ko) was a staple of the Inca diet and has distinguished itself as one of the few Andean crops to increase its range markedly in the last century. In the high Andes, from Venezuela to Chile and northwestern Argentina, it has become an important crop, particularly at altitudes between 6,000 and 12,000 feet. Along with potatoes, it is a major carbohydrate source in some areas. Enough Peruvians consider ulluco a delicacy that it is sold in modern packaging in supermarkets, with annual demand estimated at more than 60,000 tons.

The plant is unusual in that it forms tubers both above and below the ground. Frequently mistaken for fruits, the aerial tubers hang from slender stems and as they grow may eventually take root and bury themselves. Beneath the ground, ulluco forms a mass of fibrous roots whose ends thicken and swell into tubers of varied shapes and colors, the most common being spherical and golden yellow. Their thin, soft skin need not be peeled before cooking, and the flesh, normally yellow and mucilaginous, is usually prepared like potatoes and used as a thickener for soups and stews. Ulluco leaves are also edible and taste like New Zealand spinach. A close relative commonly grown in the tropics is known, in fact, by the name "malabar spinach."

Andean farmers like ulluco because it resists frost, heat, and disease. Yields average two to four tons per acre, the higher tonnages being taken in cool, moist environments. This old crop remains virtually unknown outside the Andes but seems to show exceptional promise for temperate zones and tropical highlands. Calvin Sperling, a botanist who concentrates on little-known cultivated plants and who has studied ulluco in particular, says that "if the potato can make it around the world, so can ulluco." He has grown the plant with good results in Boston, and others have grown it in greenhouses as far north as Vancouver, Canada, and Littlehampton, England.

Two other important Andean root crops are related to flowers often found in North American yards, parks, and wildlands. The achira, or edible canna (*Canna edulis*), resembles a large-leafed lily. Its fleshy, branched roots (actually rhizomes) sometimes grow as long as a forearm and contain about 25 percent starch of an easily digestible variety. The starch is a shiny yellowish powder with exceptionally large grains, big enough to see with the naked eye.

Achira has a long history in the Andean region, baked achira ranking with roast guinea pig as one of the region's oldest traditional foods. At Huaca Prieta on the Peruvian coast, samples of achira have been excavated from strata dated at about 2500 B.C., which predates the introduction of maize and manioc to that area. Its cultivation today extends from Venezuela to northern Chile, and in much of this tremendous region the young roots are a fairly common market vegetable. Achira is also grown in other parts of the tropics, notably on the Caribbean island of St. Kitts and in Australasia. In both Java and northern Australia it has been raised commercially on a small scale, and the Australian product has been marketed as "Queensland arrowroot." In subtropical Hawaii, achira has been grown as fodder for cattle and pigs.

Nasturtiums were an Inca ornamental, and their near relative mashua (*Tropaeolum tuberosum*) is a staple Andean foodstuff at elevations where potatoes and many other tubers are unsuccessful. This frost-tolerant crop is mainly cultivated in small hillside plots in cool, moist upland valleys in Colombia, Peru, and Bolivia at altitudes of 9,000 feet and above. It is reported that Peru alone has 10,000 acres of mashua under cultivation, yielding between eight and twelve tons per acre.

The mashua plant, which has more than a hundred recognized varieties, is an herbaceous climber that produces tubers shaped like either carrots or potatoes. The tubers grown in Colombia are long, deeply furrowed, and white, sometimes pink at the ends. Those in Peru and Bolivia are yellow, although often their skins sport red or purple dots and lines. Mashua is widely cultivated as a flowering ornamental in England and the United States but, like other Inca root crops, has received little testing or recognition as a food.

Mashua is not palatable raw. Indians of the Andes cure its tubers in the sun, freeze-dry them during the cold of night, and then add them to stews or eat them separately as either baked or fried vegetables. Mashua contains 18 percent starch and twice as much protein as the average potato. Its peppery taste, like that of turnips, is not universally enjoyed, but it has the important property of being storable at room temperature for as long as six months.

In terms of public awareness or usage, these treasures of the Andes remain very much buried despite the fact that root crops are in great demand throughout the world. In recent years a handful of scientists and experimental growers in South America and elsewhere have made the first concerted efforts to bring them to light, and it is time that more of their colleagues joined in this project of rediscovery. These plants, ignored by the conquistadors more than four centuries ago, are gifts of ancient gods, and like their famous and much-traveled cousin the potato, they could become major contributors both to the world food supply and to our gustatory pleasure.

CHAPTER 8

A Brief History and Botany of Cacao

JOHN A. WEST

I is recorded that Columbus, returning from his second trip to the Americas, brought specimen plants and pods of cacao to his sponsor, King Ferdinand of Spain. Apparently the uses of cacao—the raw material for chocolate—were unknown or overlooked at the time, for most early references credit Cortés as first bringing cacao beans to Spain for royal consumption in 1528. Cortés had an advantage over Columbus in having observed the preparation of cacao drinks and having consumed them at Moctezuma's court. What pleased the Aztec nobles pleased the Spanish crown as well, and so began chocolate's ascent in the Old World.

The early history of cacao and of chocolate culture is obscure, in part because conquistadors and Catholic missionaries in Latin America destroyed records wholesale in their haste to eradicate native religious and social systems. An indication of cacao's importance endures, however, in one of the few surviving documents from the Mayas, the famous Codex Mendoza, prepared by an Aztec artist for Antonio de Mendoza, the first Spanish viceroy of Mexico. Here large sacks of cacao beans are depicted, along with honey, cotton, feathers, and gold, among the fine goods that outlying peoples paid the Aztecs by way of taxes or tribute.

Unfortunately, the voluminous archaeological literature of the region provides little reliable evidence about the domestication, cultivation, processing, or trading of cacao. Paleontological evidence is equally sparse at this stage, but recent strides toward decoding Mayan hieroglyphics hold out hope for a more complete and accurate picture in the future. One promising development was the discovery in 1984 of a well-preserved pottery container at Río Azul, Guatemala, which contains cacao residues and bears a Mayan glyph for *ka-ka-wa*, from which the Spanish word *cacao* is ultimately derived. The word the Spaniards actually heard probably was *cacahuatl*, which is from the Aztec language Nahuatl and refers directly to the cacao bean.

It is repeatedly stated in the early literature that cacao had intoxicating, hallucinogenic, and aphrodisiacal properties. As regards cacao itself, these reports are unfounded, but it was sometimes blended with other ingredients that have mind-altering effects. Since pre-Columbian times the Zapotec Indians of the Oaxaca region of Mexico have added the dried aromatic flowers of *Quararibea funebris* to a chocolate drink called *tejate* that is used in the treatment of anxiety, fever, and coughs. The flowers contain two alkaloids, funebral and funebrine, which are similar to chemicals employed as anticonvulsants in modern medicine. It is also documented that hallucinogenic mushrooms like *Psilocybe* were consumed along with cacao drinks in various Aztec and Mayan rituals.

Theobroma cacao received its scientific name from the Swedish botanist Linnaeus in 1753, the root words of the genus designation being Greek for "god" and "food." *Theobroma* is a tree genus endemic to Central and South America, principally to the upper Amazon and Orinoco river basins. Of the twenty-two species known today, only cacao is raised commercially, though others have traditionally been grown in family gardens as a source of beans and of a sugary pulp for sweets and drinks. These species hold interest for genetic research aimed at improving cacao as a crop and increasing its disease resistance. The family Sterculiaceae, to which *Theobroma* belongs, has just one other genus of major economic importance—*Cola*, the primary source of flavor and caffeine for cola drinks. *Erythroxylon coca*, from which cocaine is derived, is sometimes confused with cacao and coconuts but bears no relation botanically or chemically either to *Theobroma cacao* or to the coconut palm *Cocos nucifera*.

In their crowded natural habitat of the primary rainforest, cacao trees are sparsely branched and lanky, reaching heights of fifty feet or so, whereas in unshaded plantations they branch densely and rarely stand more than a third as tall. The trees retain their leaves year-round, with new leaves developing in periodic flushes, appearing at branch tips and quickly turning from a delicate pinkish green to a deep green on the upper surface and a soft, silvery green on the lower surface, which is covered with tiny hairs. Mature leaves are elliptical and large, as much as twenty inches long, and are arrayed alternately in two rows on the branches.

After two or three years, a tree produces small, white to pink flowers in clusters on the main trunk and largest branches. Pollination of the unscented flowers is generally carried out by a small, mosquito-like midge fly, and less than 5 percent of the flowers yield fully developed pods. In its prime, an average tree brings forth twenty to fifty pods, ranging in color when ripe from yellow-green to red. Each pod contains as many as fifty beans, enough to make a hundred-gram chocolate bar. The fresh beans taste quite bitter and unpleasant, but the sweet-sour flavor and inviting aroma of the surrounding white pulp attract birds, monkeys, and other animals that open the pods, eat the pulp, and discard the seeds—a rather effective means of seed dispersal in the wild.

By the time Cortés arrived, as the Codex Mendoza makes clear, cacao was being transported in sizable quantities to the Aztec capital, and it probably was traded throughout the empire to some extent. Indian farmers, principally in the Yucatán, seem to have succeeded in bringing cacao under cultivation by this point, managing the wild crop to improve production or perhaps even raising trees from seed on the first cacao plantations. Incontrovertible evidence of such advanced cacao production is lacking, but the level of trade that occurred after the Spanish conquest seems improbable without some prior base of cacao cultivation.

As the conquistadors extended Spanish rule in Meso-america, Spanish colonial governments took over much of the prosperous Mayan agriculture and trade, thereby establishing a monopoly on cacao production. During the sixteenth and early seventeenth centuries, cacao became the Spaniards' most important export crop, and they controlled its trade and consumption in Europe as well as in their colonies. The precious beans were actually used as a currency in Central America as late as the eighteenth century.

To expand this lucrative trade, the Spanish exported cacao seedlings to many other areas. Fernando Po, a small island that lies near the equator a few miles off the coast of western Africa, became the first site of cacao cultivation outside Latin America when young plants from Venezuela took root there in 1590. Fernando Po was well chosen for cacao cultivation, for commercial production of the crop is restricted to the equatorial tropics. Usually cacao grows best at altitudes below 1,500 feet, which qualified Fernando Po in its entirety. The island's rich, well-drained soil, plentiful rainfall, and warm temperatures also proved ideal, and Fernando Po went on to serve as a springboard for cacao in Africa. Today known as Bioko, the island is part of the nation of Equatorial Guinea, and it produces 8,000 tons of cacao beans annually, generating about 70 percent of the country's export earnings.

The Spanish spread cacao west from the Americas as well. Ever since Pedro de Laguna transported cacao seedlings from Acapulco to Manila on a Spanish galleon in 1663, chocolate has been a traditional food throughout the Philippines. Today on many of its islands, families grow several cacao trees in their yards or in small orchards with other tree crops such as mangoes or bananas, using the dried beans at home or selling them in the local markets. There is also a flourishing commercial cacao industry for the domestic and export markets.

Contemporary Filipinos prepare cacao at home by methods virtually identical to those that the Spanish used in sixteenth-century Mexico. To make chocolate disks for hot drinks, they roast the beans in a wok over a wood or gas fire until the shells can be removed. The beans are then rolled and crushed lightly with a wooden roller or glass bottle and finally winnowed on a rattan tray to separate the shells from the bean fragments (nibs). The shells are fed to the chickens, the pods to pigs or goats. The nibs are ground in a corn mill (like a meat grinder) to make a warm paste that is punched into two-inch disks with a metal cutter and placed on a banana leaf to cool.

These disks, usually pure chocolate, also may be sold in the local market if they are not used at home to make hot chocolate or *champorado*, a delicious dessert and breakfast dish consisting of warm sticky-rice sweetened with sugar and flavored with the chocolate. The hot chocolate, too, is excellent and is made by traditional methods: water is boiled with sugar in a clay pot, then a chocolate disk is added and the mixture is whipped into a thick foam with a *molinillo*, a wooden stick with a fluted head.

Throughout most of its post-Mayan history, chocolate has primarily been served as a drink, hot or cold, but unlike the Filipinos, Europeans customarily adulterated cacao with other ingredients that would nauseate those who appreciate the rich and distinctive aromas and flavors of a fine, pure chocolate. Richard Cadbury's classic text *Cocoa: All About It*, published in 1896, lists the ingredients used by Spanish royalty around 1600: "hundred kernels of cocoa, two grains of chile peppers, handful of anis, dozen almonds and dozen hazelnuts, achiotte, sugar, vanilla, musk, ambergris, cinnamon, pod of campeche, powdered white roses and orange water." Of these fourteen items, only vanilla and chili peppers were flavorings used by the Aztecs, while ten of the remaining number originated in the Middle East and Southeast Asia.

Presumably the Spanish court took such great liberties in doctoring chocolate drinks because long, damp voyages from the New World left many of the beans moldy and poor tasting; the additional flavors became necessary to mask the undesirable ones. Evidently, coloring was found to be necessary as well, for achiotte and campeche are red-brown vegetable dyes. Native to Latin America, they would lend an unnatural red tinge to the rich dark brown of roasted cacao, and today they are used principally in foods other than chocolate. The Spanish may have resorted to the dyes to darken Criollo cacao, a light-colored variety from Mexico that they may have considered too pale for the kingly consumer.

As fashionable as chocolate became among European royalty, the manner in which it was conveyed from country to country on the Continent is not well documented. A merchant named Antonio Carletti is reputed to have introduced chocolate to Italy in 1606, but it is also evident that Catholic friars enjoyed the privilege of drinking hot chocolate from an early date, and they contributed to its dispersion throughout Europe as they traveled between monasteries.

French interest in chocolate was bolstered in the early seventeenth century through a series of marriages between members of the Spanish and French royal families. Undertaken to promote international relations, the marital alliances had the unintended effect of stimulating an appreciation of chocolate in the court at Versailles. French interest in the American novelty was cemented in 1660 when Marie-Thérèse of Spain, a chocolate enthusiast of the first order, married Louis XIV. The pastry chefs of Paris never looked back.

Precisely when or in what form cacao first reached England's shores is not documented, but perhaps it came directly across the English Channel, for London's first chocolate house, opened in 1657, was run by a Frenchman. Like the coffee houses established a few years earlier, chocolate houses rapidly increased in number and became centers of political, economic, and social debate for the wealthy and powerful.

As demand for cacao grew in the seventeenth and eighteenth centuries, the French led an assault on the Spanish agricultural and trade monopolies in cacao, beginning active cacao production in their own Caribbean possessions of Martinique and St. Lucia around 1660. The French expanded into the Brazilian state of Bahia in 1746, inaugurating cultivation there of this crop native to the nearby Amazon basin.

The Dutch followed suit, getting their start in cacao production, it appears, through illicit commerce between the natives of Mindanao, in the Philippines, and Java, in what was then the Dutch East Indies. A fierce Dutch–Spanish trade rivalry precluded trade between these colonial outposts, but the covert flow of cacao seedlings out of the Philippines was sufficient to make possible the establishment of an experimental cacao garden in Jakarta. In 1778 the Dutch Batavian Society of Arts and Sciences offered a silver medal to the first person to plant fifty cacao trees successfully, and subsequently cacao agriculture became quite profitable in both Sumatra and Java despite major problems with insect pests. Dutch government biologists, in combination with local farmers, provided a very satisfactory agricultural base, and thanks to this colonial legacy, the nation of Indonesia now produces 75,000 tons of cacao beans each year.

The harvesting and initial treatment of the beans has changed little over the centuries. Pods are carefully cut from the tree with a machete or a special knife to avoid damaging the flower cushion. Within a day or two after harvesting, the pods are opened with a machete or a small splitting blade embedded in a wood block. In a few areas, gas-powered pod-splitting machines are now in use to reduce hand labor.

The wet beans and white pulp are placed in large, square wooden boxes for fermentation by yeasts and bacteria that obtain their nutrients from sugars and other compounds in the pulp. In the five to seven days that the fermentation continues, the bean mass heats up, reaching temperatures as high as 50°C (120°F) and prompting a complex of organic chemical changes. This process kills the beans and alters their carbohydrates, proteins, and pigments, changing the beans' color from purple to brown. These are the first, essential steps in chocolate making; without such fermentation, the beans do not attain full flavor.

Following fermentation, the beans are spread to dry on sunlit platforms, and there they are raked and turned several times daily for three to five days. Sometimes drying is accelerated with rotary dryers that burn wood or petroleum, but sun drying yields the best flavor. By the time the beans are packed for storage and shipment, they are only about 5 percent water and must be kept dry. If their moisture content rises above 7 percent, secondary fungal contamination occurs, spoiling the flavor and reducing the beans' value considerably.

While few improvements have been made in the basic methods of processing cacao beans, much has changed in the preparation and consumption of chocolate. Water, coffee, and even wine and beer were used as bases for chocolate drinks during the early European period. It was only in 1727 that an Englishman named Nicholas Sanders first blended chocolate with milk to produce the hot chocolate of which the Western world has become so fond. Special credit for promoting this concoction is due to Sir Hans Sloane, a British physician who recommended it as particularly healthful for children and praised "its lightness on the stomach and its great use in consumptive cases."

Walter Churchman of Bristol started the first chocolate manufacturing in Britain in about 1728, and by 1761, Joseph Fry, a Quaker, had taken over the business. Soon afterward, two other Quaker families, the Cadburys and the Rowntrees, got into the chocolate trade, launching business empires that dominated this food line in Britain and the Commonwealth for more than two hundred years. Cadbury Brothers acquired the rights and the label for "Sir Hans Sloane's Milk Chocolate prepared after the original recipe." The directions were simple: "Put one ounce of chocolate to a pint of boiling milk, add sugar."

The use of cocoa in the Royal Navy is known to Anglophiles and chocophiles alike because hot chocolate assumed an importance as great as the more traditional daily issue of rum. Captain James Ferguson, stationed in Antigua, first introduced cacao to vessels in the West Indies in about 1780, emphasizing both its nutritional value and its low cost. This ration, known first as the cocoa issue, then as CI or "kye," soon spread throughout the British fleet. By the middle of the nineteenth century, at least half the cacao imported into Great Britain was allotted to the Royal Navy to be issued as sugar-sweetened slabs of hard chocolate. Until 1968, when the bars were finally replaced by cocoa powder, the sailors made hot chocolate by mixing chocolate shavings with hot water and condensed milk.

Hot chocolate's popularity at sea, in chocolate houses, and at home gave rise to the manufacture of elaborate gold, silver, pewter, and porcelain chocolate pots and services. Made in England and throughout Europe, these finely crafted pieces of cacao paraphernalia were each equipped with a swizzle stick to whip the heavy chocolate. While their forerunners, ornate tea and coffee services, still see use in high society, chocolate pots swiftly disappeared from the scene with the advent in 1828 of hydraulic presses to extract cacao butter, a development that brought cocoa powder into extensive use for the first time. Often quite beautiful, chocolate services today command sums as great as $50,000 on the antique market.

Like other New World commodities that captured the taste buds of Europe, chocolate left its mark on the fine arts as well as on crafts. In the late seventeenth century, painters began taking chocolate as a subject, depicting its consumption by people of all classes but especially by the aristocracy, and these canvases furnish insights into the social and private lives of the times. The most illustrious example comes from the hand of Jean-Étienne Liotard, a Swiss artist who was commissioned in 1743 to execute a portrait of the Austrian empress Maria Theresa and her family. While Liotard stayed in Vienna to do the painting, he was served breakfast chocolate each day by a certain chambermaid. The charm of this woman and the tastiness of her offerings so entranced him that she became the subject of his most famous painting, *La Belle Chocolatière*.

Interest in chocolate came later to the North American colonies than to Europe, and its availability was correspondingly slow to develop. The Dutch in New Amsterdam (now New York) were still obtaining their cacao from Holland in the early eighteenth century, and Boston apothecaries did not advertise chocolate as a remedy ("confection") until 1712. By the middle of the century, however, New England shipping was carrying cargoes of cacao beans and rum from the Caribbean, and in 1786 Thomas Jefferson was quoted as predicting, "The superiority of chocolate for health and nourishment, will soon give it the same preference over tea and coffee in America that it has in Spain."

Chocolate production in North America got its start in 1765 when John Hannon established the nation's first chocolate mill on the Neponset River in what is now Dorchester, Massachusetts—also probably the only U.S. chocolate factory ever to grind its beans by waterpower. After Hannon was lost at sea on a trading voyage to the Caribbean, Dr. James Baker became a financial partner in the company, and it adopted his name in 1779. More than two centuries later, Baker Chocolate remains an important name in the American chocolate industry, and Liotard's *Belle Chocolatière*, which graces its label, is today the most widely recognized chocolate symbol in the United States.

Cacao agriculture continued to expand in the nineteenth and twentieth centuries. In 1836, Spanish and German colonists significantly increased production in Bahia, beginning a boom in cacao that has made Brazil a great chocolate power, the world's second largest cacao producer at present. The famous twentieth-century Brazilian author Jorge Amado has immortalized the earthy, often violent life of Bahia's nineteenth-century *cacaoeiros* (cacao farmers) in four novels, of which *Dona Flor and Her Two Husbands* is the best known, having also been successful as a movie.

The islands of São Tomé and Principe, which served as ports of call for Portuguese slave vessels in the period between 1550 and 1750, also became cacao-producing giants. Lying just to the south of Fernando Po, these colonies received their first cacao plants from Brazil in about 1825 and soon moved the Portuguese into competition with Spain, France, and Holland. Between 1895 and 1910 the islands ranked fifth in world production, trading over 30,000 tons of beans each year. By 1890, however, the British and German chocolate manufacturers were boycotting São Tomé and Principe because slave labor was used on their cacao plantations. Today their cacao yield has declined to about 4,000 tons, but this harvest provides the São Tomé–Principe microstate with 80 percent of its export revenue.

Ghana appears to have been the first country of mainland Africa in which full-scale cacao cultivation was attempted. As early as 1857 the Danish Basel Mission in Ghana obtained a few seedlings from Surinam, but none of these survived. In subsequent efforts during the next twenty years, the mission met with repeated failure as plant disease, pests, and theft resulted in the loss of trees and pods. At the same time, however, other new crops such as coffee succeeded among local farmers, and finally, in the late 1870s, cacao was launched with pods and seeds obtained from Cameroon and elsewhere.

Ghana gives principal credit for the origin of its cacao agriculture to the larger-than-life figure of Teteh Quashie, a blacksmith who worked for several years as a transient laborer in a cacao plantation on Fernando Po. Quashie is reputed to have returned to Ghana with some pods, started a cacao nursery around 1881, and sold pods for one British pound each to local farmers interested in broadening their economic base. Several public buildings and memorials now honor Quashie as a national hero.

Ghana had become a British colony in 1874, remaining so until 1957, and British influence contributed to the agricultural success the nation achieved prior to its independence. Ghana not only took the lead in African cacao production but bypassed New World producers to achieve world supremacy with yields exceeding 400,000 tons per annum. For years, cacao from Ghana also set the industry standard for basic chocolate flavor because the beans were particularly well fermented and cured, and it has dominated the British and European markets for much of the twentieth century. In 1981 a change of government brought a drastic decline in cacao production, but in recent years yields have increased again.

At present, the Ivory Coast is the world's leading cacao producer, harvesting 750,000 tons of dried beans annually. In Latin America, Brazil heads the list with 350,000 tons a year, followed by the Dominican Republic, Ecuador, Colombia, Venezuela, and Mexico. In the Far East, Malaysia yields 275,000 tons per annum, and along with Indonesia, Papua New Guinea has become a significant producer. Growth of the worldwide output, which exceeded 2.4 million tons in 1990, has caused a sharp decline in cacao prices, dropping the value of beans on the New York and London futures markets from over $2,000 a ton to less than half that amount. Growers generally receive less than 50 percent of the market price.

Chocolate's nutritional and psychological value has made it an excellent source of sustenance not only for British seamen but also for climbers and adventurers of other kinds. It drew great attention in this respect as a ration for Antarctic expeditions in the early twentieth century. Pure chocolate is more than half cocoa butter, which has a very high energy output per unit of weight, much higher than protein- and carbohydrate-rich foods. This important consideration made it a logical selection for sled travel across the polar snow and ice, and virtually all the expeditions carried it in quantity. Roland Huntford has calculated that chocolate may have been a deciding factor between Roald Amundsen's successful trek to the South Pole and the fatal attempt led by Robert Scott. Scott allocated his men only 4,430 calories per day, including twenty-four grams of cocoa, whereas the Amundsen party completed the trek in good health with daily rations of 4,560 calories that featured five times as much cocoa.

Huntford quotes a succinct account of the Amundsen team's return to home base from its polar exploits:

> Have you been there? Yes, we've been there, answered Roald Amundsen, and there was a hullabaloo. Soon after, we were all seated round the table and savoured Lindstrom's hot cakes and heavenly coffee. How good a cup of coffee can really taste one only realizes when, like us, one has had to go without so long.

"That statement came from the heart," comments Huntford: "for ninety-nine days the Polar party had drunk nothing but chocolate."

The sturdy wooden hut built on Ross Island in the Antarctic for the 1907–1909 Shackleton Expedition to the South Pole still stands as an international heritage site, its original contents intact. These include pound and half-pound canisters of Fry's Pure Concentrated Cocoa and Rowntree's Select Cocoa, along with Heinz India Relish and Colman's Mustard. The cocoa appears to be unaffected by its many decades on the shelf and has a flavor equal to that of today's products—

persuasive testimony to both the preservative properties of the Antarctic climate and the durable virtues of chocolate.

Chocolate has won a place in modern literature as well as in outdoor life. Amado's Bahian novels and Roald Dahl's _Charlie and the Chocolate Factory_ are contemporary examples, but perhaps the greatest is still British playwright George Bernard Shaw's _Arms and the Man,_ written in 1894. Set amidst a battle between the Serbian and Russian armies, the story involves a Swiss mercenary officer serving with the Serbs who flees the heat of combat and finds refuge in the home of a lovely young woman, whose father happens to be fighting on the Russian side. Although the Swiss officer carries a revolver, he confesses that he has no bullets because he chose to carry chocolate instead of extra ammunition. Worse yet, he has exhausted his chocolate supply. His protector offers him the last of her chocolate creams, which he eagerly accepts, but she castigates him for being a "chocolate cream soldier," and the play unfolds with further chocolate drama.

This brief account of modern chocolate culture would be incomplete without reference to contemporary chocolate-centered celebrations of St. Valentine's Day and Easter. It is unclear precisely when the custom developed of commemorating these dates with chocolate, but the tradition has been well established in Europe and the United States for many years and is taking hold in other parts of the world. The Valentine season now brings peak chocolate sales not only in the United States but also in Japan, where it has become a business obligation for women to present gifts of candy to their male colleagues on February 14. The result is a merchandising bonanza worth some $350 million a year, with boxes of really elegant Japanese chocolates selling for as much as three hundred dollars.

Molded chocolate Easter eggs and bunnies have become

popular especially in the past century and are particularly appropriate because springtime, rabbits, and eggs are all linked with rituals of fertility in European history. Adding this to the frenzy of chocolate consumption on Valentine's Day, one has cause to wonder if there is more to chocolate's ancient reputation as an aphrodisiac than science has yet detected. At this point, all that has been demonstrated is a connection between the psychology of romance and various amines, such as phenylethylamine. These compounds, present in chocolate but also in many other foods, play an important role in human neurological functions.

Whatever factors may be driving it, no end is in sight for the boom in chocolate appreciation. The consumption of chocolate is increasing at the rate of 3 to 4 percent each year, and annual intake per person has reached strikingly high levels in affluent countries. Switzerland presently leads the world, with sales of about nineteen pounds per capita, although this statistic is surely inflated by large tourist purchases of the outstanding Swiss candies. The Norwegians and British follow, consuming an average of seventeen and a half pounds of chocolate annually. Next come the Belgians, Dutch, western Germans, and Austrians, who all average more than fourteen pounds each year. U.S. residents weigh in at ten pounds per capita, so evidently chocolate is not a principal contributor to our problems as an overweight nation. The annual intake of the slender Japanese is only three pounds, and that of Latin American citizens is still lower.

New chocolate products continue to appear on the market in remarkable diversity. In the United States, Britain, Thailand, and other countries, for instance, high-fat cacao powder is added to the leaves of another American native plant, tobacco, in the interest of improving the flavor of cigarettes. Shopkeepers in Korea offer another novel chocolate product—"Cacao," a brand of chewing gum. This too is a doubly American commodity, for the gum base comes from a rubbery exudate of the sapodilla tree (*Achras sapote*), which the Mayas were chewing many centuries ago. Though the chewing quality of "Cacao" is excellent, its chocolate flavoring appears to be synthetic.

Unfortunately, there is a serious underside to chocomania's continued advance: efforts to increase cacao production may hasten clearing of the world's already dwindling tropical rainforests, essential bastions of biological diversity. An alternative to destroying the rainforests is now being tested in Hawaii: the conversion of small sugarcane and pineapple plantations to cacao. If pilot projects succeed, this approach will provide a means not only of easing the pressure on tropical rainforests but also of easing the conscience of those of us who love to eat chocolate.

CHAPTER 9

Quinoa's Roundabout Journey to World Use

JOHN F. MCCAMANT

I n 1582, Spanish colonial administrators distributed a questionnaire asking, "What are the seeds, plants,
and green vegetables which serve or have served as food for
the aborigines?" The answer came back from the Andes that
quinoa was second only to potatoes as food, with maize (corn)
in third place. Nearly three decades later, Garcilaso de la Vega,
an Inca émigré in Spain, confirmed the prominence of quinoa
in his *Royal Commentaries of the Incas*, writing, "The second
most important of the crops which are grown above ground
[after maize] is that called quinua or in Spanish 'millet' or
'little rice,' which it rather resembles in the color and appearance of the grain." Note that Garcilaso, who had left Peru
when he was twenty, reverses the ranking of maize and quinoa.
In doing so, he may have expressed a bias of his new country, for Spaniards took great interest in maize, which grew
well at the altitudes where they preferred to live, but virtually
ignored quinoa, which favors the higher, cooler environments
inhabited by the majority of the Inca population.

Four hundred and fifty years later, it seems strange indeed that the Spanish took so little interest in this exceptional plant. Dazzlingly beautiful in the field, it grows successfully in many environments inhospitable to other crops. Rich in flavor and supremely versatile in its uses, quinoa is among the most nutritious of all grains. This unclaimed treasure of the Andes remains available thanks to generations of indigenous farmers working fields their North American counterparts would consider too small or steep to till. Even in the past forty years, since its value was recognized by science, a series of political and agricultural obstacles have impeded quinoa from taking its natural place in the world's food basket.

The small grain of *Chenopodium quinoa* grows on a plant whose broad leaves take the shape of a goose foot. At maturity, atop stalks three to seven feet tall, its sorghum-like seed-heads turn brilliant shades of red, white, yellow, or black before they dry out and are ready for harvesting. The plant is closely related to spinach and beets and even more closely related to a worldwide weed known in English as lamb's-quarters. A number of quinoa's wild relatives in the chenopod genus cross quite readily with the cultivated plant.

Quinoa has been called a pseudo-cereal because it does not belong to the grass family, as wheat, oats, and most other grains do. Those of us who work with quinoa prefer to class it as a leafy grain, along with amaranth and buckwheat, not only to avoid negative nomenclature but also to call attention to the fact that the leaves of these plants are valuable food sources. Quinoa seed contains a nearly perfect balance of essential amino acids, including lysine, which runs short in the grassy grains. Its protein level ranges as high as 22 percent and averages about 16 percent, compared to wheat's 12 percent. Quinoa also supplies substantial amounts of iron, calcium, and vitamins B and E. The grain has little vitamin A, but the edible leaf has it in abundance. In short, the quinoa plant can satisfy all of a person's basic nutritional needs.

Quinoa has the telltale properties of a long-cultivated plant, including an inability, under normal circumstances, to survive in the wild. Its seeds mature all at once and do not shatter, traits that make the grain easy to harvest and that native planters probably promoted by the selection and preservation of seed down through the centuries. The seed's thin coat and lack of dormancy also give it the quality of germinating very quickly when exposed to moisture, which is desirable as long as farmers husband the seed carefully but means that quinoa left to stand in the fields will sprout in the fall, sometimes right on the stalk, and be killed by winter temperatures.

Archaeological evidence indicates that quinoa was cultivated as early as 5800 to 4500 B.C. in the Ayacucho basin of Peru and was being traded by 1000 to 900 B.C. along the coast of what is now Chile. Archaeologist David Browman has found that quinoa comprises 70 to 90 percent of the seeds excavated from a site at Chiripa near Lake Titicaca, a site that dates from the period 1350 B.C. to A.D. 50. Evidently, quinoa was a staple in this high plateau, and Browman notes an increase in seed size at Chiripa after 1000 B.C., a clear sign of the crop's domestication and improvement. A closely related chenopod still found in the wild has been unearthed at several archaeological excavations in the eastern United States and has now been established as one of the first agricultural crops within the borders of the present nation, dating from about two thousand years ago and thus preceding maize by several hundred years.

Until recently it was generally accepted that quinoa originated in the Lake Titicaca region because that was the area of greatest diversity for the plant. Texas A&M botanist Hugh Wilson threw some doubt on that conclusion in 1979, however, when he found a wild North American species with a genetic structure similar to quinoa's. Humberto Gandarillas, the grandfather of quinoa research in Bolivia, took up the challenge and sought possible wild precursors of quinoa in the vicinity of La Paz. Crossing several wild chenopods, he found one hybrid that produced fertile offspring with the characteristics of quinoa, including the shape of its seedhead and the color and size of the seed. He concluded that quinoa could have originated in any of the valleys of Peru or Bolivia where both these apparent progenitors are found in the wild.

In any case, quinoa spread throughout South America to an area that closely coincided with the extent of the Inca empire. Its northernmost reach was the Sabana of Bogotá in Colombia, and its southern limit was the Isla de Chiloé, two-thirds of the way down the coast of Chile. Peruvian agronomist Mario Tapia has identified four general types of quinoa, corresponding to the ecological niches in which they are found. A great deal of variation exists within each of these ecotypes, but they provide a sense of the adaptability and prehistoric range of the plant. Valley quinoa grows in the valleys of Peru, Ecuador, eastern Bolivia, and southern Colombia at elevations from 7,000 to 13,000 feet. These tall, slow-maturing varieties are usually planted in association with maize at the lower elevations and with potatoes and barley at the higher elevations. Altiplano quinoa grows above 12,000 feet in Peru and Bolivia and also in parts of northern Argentina and Chile. It is a smaller plant than valley quinoa, quicker to mature and more often cultivated alone in small plots. The salt-flats quinoa of southern Bolivia grows at altitudes of 10,000 to 12,000 feet, has a medium maturing time, and produces somewhat larger seeds than other types. Finally, sea-level quinoa is found along the coast of southern Chile. It has a medium maturing time and resembles the altiplano ecotype in size, but most varieties have a translucent starch not found in higher-elevation quinoa.

Its range and nutritive value made quinoa the basis for the great pre-Columbian civilizations of the Andes. The cultural center of Tiahuanaco, which flourished from A.D. 600 to 1200, was particularly dependent on quinoa because maize would not grow at its 12,497-foot location on the shores of Lake Titicaca. The Inca empire, which succeeded Tiawanaco in governing the area, was centered at Cuzco, 1,300 feet lower, and thus was able to rely on both quinoa and maize. Until the Spanish conquest, two-thirds of the population of what is now Peru lived in quinoa-growing areas of the sierra.

The ancient Andean people ate the grain boiled alone or with herbs, ground it into flour for cakes, cooked the green leaves as a potherb, and drank the fermented grain in a kind of beer. They also used the plant for non-nutritive purposes—employing the seeds' bitter coat of saponin for soap, ashes of the stalks to bring out the powers of coca, and unwashed grain as a medicine. The Incas called it the "mother grain" and held it sacred. Each year, the Inca ruler planted the first quinoa seeds of the season, using a golden foot-plow, and priests offered it to the sun in vases of gold at the solstice.

Many theories can be proposed for the Spaniards' failure to adopt quinoa. They brought to the New World their own grains—rye, barley, oats, and wheat—as well as sheep and cattle. Potatoes complemented these foods, but the well-balanced protein of quinoa was of scant importance, given the abundance of meat produced by extensive ranching on lands that had swiftly become depopulated. Quinoa also lacked the gluten needed to make yeasted bread, the mainstay of the European diet, and if the quinoa samples tasted by the newcomers had not been thoroughly cleansed of their bitter coat of saponin, the Spaniards could easily have failed to appreciate its fine flavor. Last but not least, the Spaniards may have directly suppressed the cultivation of quinoa because of its religious significance to the indigenous population.

In any event, what the Spaniards did not adopt, they ruined. The sophisticated, highly productive agricultural system of the Incas and their predecessors was allowed to fall apart. Complex patterns of cooperation and labor exchange that had been developed to maintain the agricultural infrastructure of roads, terraces, and irrigation works could no longer be sustained by a population drastically reduced by epidemics and forced to divert much of its labor into mining and other economic activities demanded by the Spanish.

In the 1570s, resettlement of the indigenous population into *reducciones* (an early version of "strategic hamlets") facilitated colonial control and labor recruitment and further hampered the collective work needed to preserve the farming infrastructure. Within a hundred years, the population of the sierra, although holding up better than peoples of the coastal regions, dropped to a sixth of the preconquest level. Quinoa lapsed along with the society and agricultural system that had nurtured it. Remnants of the agricultural system remained in the indigenous villages, however, and there quinoa continued to be grown.

To reverse this trend, in the last forty years a small but burgeoning group of Andean researchers has investigated and promoted the use of quinoa and other pre-Columbian crops. With support from international agencies and foreign governments, South American agronomists collected quinoa specimens and built good seed banks in Ecuador, Peru, and Bolivia; bred improved varieties; identified optimum levels of fertilizer application; found pesticides for various insects that infest quinoa fields; and devised improved harvesting techniques. Engineers assisted the endeavor by designing low-cost machinery for removing saponin and by making this technology available to villages, while nutritionists analyzed quinoa's food value and began actively promoting its use. The South American private sector also stepped in and started to market quinoa, the most notable firm in the field being Inca Sur, which merchandises a line of whole grain, flour, and rolled flakes from its base in the ancient Inca capital of Cuzco in Peru.

One of the primary motivations for promoting quinoa and improving its cultivation in South America has been to improve the nutrition of the high-elevation population, most of which is indigenous. The 1948 UN-sponsored nutritional conference that first recommended investigating quinoa suggested that the crop could "play a major role in feeding the Upland Indians, whose nutrition problems are among the most serious in the Americas." When the National Academy of Sciences in the United States added its voice to the call for quinoa research in 1975, it too sounded this theme, pointing out that "its grain, rich in protein and containing a good amino acid balance, may prove to be a better protein source than most of the true [that is, grassy] cereals. In the high Andes, quinua is primarily a food of campesinos and poorer classes; increasing quinua production and use could improve their inadequate diet."

Seventeen years later, it seems clear that these well-meaning scholars misinterpreted the problem. Native populations certainly knew all about quinoa, and their organic farming techniques, handed down from their pre-Columbian ancestors, have proved to be among the best in the world. Quinoa has endured among them because it co-evolved with their societies and thus fits their needs precisely. For instance, in Nuñoa, a mountain valley above Lake Titicaca, native farmers continue to plant quinoa and its close relative, the even more cold-tolerant kaniwa. Anthropologist R. Brooke Thomas, studying the area in the 1970s, observed that Old World grains grown there were "more susceptible than Andean grains to frost, hail, and snow" and calculated that the Andean grains had far and away the highest energy efficiency of the food produced, much higher than that of livestock. Computing energy efficiency as the ratio of energy obtained to energy expended, Thomas found that quinoa yielded 50 percent more energy than potatoes per unit of land. Civilization could not survive in this harsh, cold climate without the Andean grains.

The peasant population of southern Bolivia's barren salt flats is even more dependent on quinoa than the people of Nuñoa because their land lacks enough moisture to grow potatoes except in very limited areas of irrigation. Quinoa not only will grow with just five to ten inches of rainfall annually but also tolerates salty, alkaline soils. These characteristics have enabled farmers from the salt flats to succeed in taking more than a bare subsistence from their unpromising land. They are among the few native quinoa farmers who sell as much as half their production for cash. Their cooperative, Operación Tierra, holds an annual quinoa festival and is one of the most energetic promoters of quinoa in the world.

Resorting to the capital-intensive, chemical-dependent agricultural techniques encouraged by the internationally supported research would boost quinoa yields in indigenous fields, but there has been little market for quinoa because the more affluent Spanish-speaking whites and mestizos of low-lying areas disdained it. Cash-poor South American governments, recognizing the value of their indigenous crops and having a need to expand domestic food resources, have addressed this part of the quinoa problem with publicity and motivational campaigns. The Bolivian government, for example, began promoting quinoa in the mid 1970s, even passing a law that required bread to contain a minimum of 5 percent quinoa flour. Bolivian acreage planted in quinoa nearly doubled between 1970 and 1977 but returned to its former level two years later as bakers resisted and the law went unenforced. Undaunted by this failure, the government has continued to support a quinoa revival within its extremely stringent budgetary limits.

Quinoa research and development followed a different path in Chile, where the promotion of indigenous food and culture was an important part of the socialist program of Salvador Allende, elected president in 1970. With this inspiration, researchers at the University of Concepción began working on quinoa and proposed the construction of a pilot plant to process quinoa and make flour. The work was hardly launched, however, when the CIA, in league with rightist Chilean forces, precipitated a military coup that ended the Allende government. The ensuing military dictatorship suspended all work on quinoa, instead subsidizing production of wheat. Since quinoa and wheat compete for the same land in central and southern Chile, the promotion of wheat hastened the decline of quinoa. In 1981, botanist Hugh Wilson found it "on the road to extinction in south-central Chile. Cultivation is declining, and many of the younger informants showed disdain for the crop; in many instances, germplasm and information were available only from the most senior individuals of a given family unit."

To this day, the Spanish-speaking middle classes of South America continue largely to reject quinoa, spurning it as an Indian food, and it is rarely served at the restaurants of the two major cities in the center of quinoa production, Puno, Peru, and La Paz, Bolivia. One has to go into the Indian markets to find it. For quinoa to gain broad acceptance in South America, this deeply held bias against the grain must be overcome. Increased nationalist appreciation of the Indian heritage would certainly help, but such is the power of North American trends that for quinoa the shortest route from Peru's highlands to its lowland capital, as one Peruvian researcher laughingly suggested in the early 1980s, may prove to be through the U.S. health-food market.

Even this route has been full of detours and roadblocks. Introducing a new crop into a modern industrialized nation is no small task. Soybeans were successfully established in the United States in the 1930s, but this Asian crop had very strong support from the U.S. Department of Agriculture, which spent thirty million 1930s dollars to secure its present place in the affections of the nation's farmers. More recently and on a much smaller scale, amaranth has obtained a foothold in North America with little government cooperation, but it has had creative and energetic sponsorship from the Rodale Institute. Quinoa has not yet found such well-endowed or well-placed supporters and has received almost no funding in this country. Its limited success thus far has resulted from the dedication of a small group of people joined in a loose network, all doing their part with few resources and often without pay in the belief that it is time to accept, even embrace, this gift from the great civilizations of South America.

Much of the credit for getting quinoa started in the United States belongs to three men—Stephen Gorad, Don McKinley, and David Cusack—who, with scant background in the subject, accepted the challenge that agricultural experts had declined. Gorad and McKinley learned of quinoa in 1977 while studying in Boston with the Bolivian founder of the Arica Institute, Oscar Ichazo, who let it be known that quinoa was "a very nutritious food which is good to eat while doing mystical work." Gorad, who had taken a doctoral degree in psychology, got his first taste of the grain while visiting Bolivia in 1977 and promptly fell in love with it. Interested in the relation between food and holistic health, he brought quinoa back to the United States and served it to all his friends, including McKinley, a businessman whose prior enterprises included importing South American crafts. The two decided to try importing quinoa but could not figure out how to acquire it in sufficient quantity.

Gorad and McKinley introduced Cusack to quinoa in 1981, and he soon allied himself with the cause of bringing it to the United States. It was a mission for which he seemed, in some respects, particularly well suited. A political scientist with a special interest in Latin America, he had been raised in the higher elevations of Colorado and there had both seen his father's potato farm frozen out and developed an affinity for Native American traditions. Furthermore, Cusack lacked any tendency toward risk aversion, telling friends he never wanted to know what he would be doing six months in the future. His fluency in Spanish and previous work on an Aspen Institute agroclimate project for South America provided him with contacts that would prove valuable in the effort to introduce quinoa to the United States. Sierra Blanca Associates, a nonprofit organization he had put together earlier in 1981, would serve as a useful vehicle for research, development, and international cooperation.

Part of the challenge this bright, overeducated, creative trio faced was that all prior attempts to raise quinoa outside South America had failed. The first recorded trial, Inca Garcilaso de la Vega's sixteenth-century effort to grow quinoa in Spain, came to naught because his seeds did not germinate. (They had probably been obtained in the market and thus had been washed and dried to remove saponin, with a resulting loss of viability.) Subsequent, more scientific attempts had done little better. When Elizabeth Eiselen surveyed the results in

1956, she concluded: "In spite of numerous attempts, [quinoa] has never been successfully introduced elsewhere. When it has been tried at high elevations in the United States, the plant has flourished during the long summer days, reaching heights of seven feet, but the seed does not mature before the plants are killed by winter cold."

Despite this record, the three friends considered it necessary to try. It was conceivable that a market for quinoa could be developed in the United States entirely on the basis of imports, in the pattern of tea, coffee, and cocoa, but for three reasons Cusack, Gorad, McKinley, and later quinoa converts found this alternative either unlikely or undesirable. The first reason was sheer economic expediency: all the major foods consumed in the industrial world are also grown domestically. Production close to home allows Northern Hemisphere manufacturers to integrate foods into their product lines with confidence that the supply is secure.

The other reasons were humanitarian or political in nature. Quinoa has the potential to provide a new means of economic development in the mountainous regions of southern Colorado and northern New Mexico, the location of some of the poorest counties in the United States. People in this area, whose struggle for livelihood was accurately depicted in John Nichols's novel *The Milagro Beanfield War* and in the movie of the same name, have little water for irrigation and few crops aside from hay that grow well in their high-elevation fields.

Finally, large-scale U.S. imports of South American quinoa might well endanger Andean indigenous communities, which are among the few where Native Americans have been able to maintain their land and traditions. The Andean communities have preserved their way of life in part because the products of their mountain plots have not yet found strong commercial markets. A high demand and price for quinoa exports could make their lands attractive to entrepreneurs, who have always managed to usurp indigenous land once it proved its value for export crops. If quinoa were to become a bonanza in the Andes, indigenous communities would encounter pressures on their diet as well as on their landholdings, as prices enticed them to sell large portions of their quinoa crop and to eat less themselves. North American production, it was believed, would prevent unintended harm to the very people who have preserved the grain down through the centuries.

Gorad was living in Santiago, Chile, when it was decided to go ahead with this venture, so the job of finding seed stock fell to him. The only seed he could find produced well that year in the group's experimental fields, which lay above 7,000 feet in the Colorado Rockies. Encouraged by this unprecedented success, Cusack traveled through South America in 1983, gathering a much wider variety of quinoa seed and purchasing the first quantities to import. An Andean crops group led by Mario Tapia, the Peruvian agronomist, cooperated fully in providing seed and information, and Tapia visited the Colorado research fields in August 1983 to see for himself that quinoa would flourish outside the Andes. Cusack, Gorad, and McKinley formed the Quinoa Corporation in 1983 and secured enough financing to begin operations in earnest in 1984.

In May of that year, after organizing the planting of the research fields in Colorado and also arranging for 160 acres of commercial fields, Cusack flew to South America to attend the Fourth Andean Crops Congress and to draft a cooperative proposal on valley quinoa with Tapia in Peru. Afterward, he went on to Bolivia and there, while visiting the ruins of Tiahuanaco, he was shot in the back by an unidentified assailant and died of internal bleeding. The murder, which seems to have been premeditated and well planned, remains unsolved.

The most credible motive for killing Cusack relates to his knowledge not of quinoa but of the CIA's successful campaign to destabilize the Allende government in Chile. At the time of his death he was contemplating a book laying out the details of CIA involvement in Chile and comparing U.S. intervention in Latin America and Indochina.

Whatever its circumstances, Cusack's murder dealt a major blow to quinoa research and development in the United States. Gorad and McKinley could follow through on the importing and distribution business of Quinoa Corporation, but of the three, only Cusack was deeply involved in growing quinoa in the United States, and he was sorely missed when a string of crop setbacks followed the initial successes of 1982 and 1983. The acreage he had obtained for commercial production in 1984, planted with an improved variety that had not previously been tested in Colorado, yielded no grain at all, and the research fields also experienced a multitude of problems.

Fortunately, trials of 150 kinds of seed did produce an answer to the question of why the commercial fields and most other quinoa plantings had utterly failed: Many quinoa varieties are sensitive to the length of the day and will not bloom until days and nights are equally long. In the mountains of the Northern Hemisphere, this seasonal constraint does not leave sufficient time for grain to mature before cold sets in. Most quinoa from southern Bolivia and from Chile, such as Gorad first happened to obtain, lacks such photoperiod sensitivity and blooms early enough in the Colorado summer to produce seed. This finding was a major breakthrough, but the year's results ruled out further commercial fields for the time being and made it clear that the development of quinoa production in Colorado was going to be much more difficult than Cusack had anticipated.

The other side of Quinoa Corporation's work went better. Using imported grain, the fledgling company sold its first quinoa at Alfalfa's Market in Boulder, Colorado, in June 1984. The firm then introduced it to health-food distributors, who are accustomed to handling small quantities of specialty foods and who found the nutritional properties of quinoa a strong selling point. Food writers helped open the way for quinoa, contributing good public exposure as they competed to "discover" this wonderful food. Rebecca Wood led off in 1985 with the first food article on quinoa published in English and followed in 1989 with the first cookbook devoted to the little chenopod, featuring recipes elegant enough to appeal to gourmet cooks and restaurant chefs. The *New York Times, Newsweek, Gourmet Magazine*, and other publications reported on the new "supergrain." Vegetarians and sufferers from wheat allergies were among the most enthusiastic early U.S. consumers of quinoa, since it expanded and enriched their diets.

All told, the Quinoa Corporation sold 11,529 pounds of quinoa in the United States in 1984. Even at the good average price of $2.25 per pound, however, these sales left little cash to cover overhead and salaries. The Quinoa Corporation struggled through two more years, but while sales increased, profits did not. To obtain needed capital, in late 1986 Gorad and McKinley sold the company to a small conglomerate, and since then it has changed hands twice more and has been moved to California. Thus by 1989 none of the three men who originally set out to introduce quinoa to the United States was still involved in the endeavor.

In the intervening period, South American entrepreneurs recognized the potential for quinoa sales to the U.S. and European markets and managed to take over the provision of quinoa to the health-food distributors Eden Foods and

Arrowhead Mills. The volume of quinoa sold has risen swiftly but is still very small by U.S. standards, amounting to only about 750 tons in 1988. Still, that figure represents a hundred-fold increase in five years' time, and this growth, along with all the plaudits from journalists, makes it hard now to consider quinoa a scorned "Indian food" of South America. With Boulder and San Francisco yuppies talking excitedly about it, could the middle classes of Quito and Lima fail to take note?

That remains to be seen, but the resilience of the peasant farmers and the four-decade campaign by Andean agricultural specialists appears to be reversing quinoa's fortunes. After an all-time low in 1979, Bolivian land in quinoa production has increased by 34 percent annually, and similar, though less spectacular, increases have occurred in other countries. The governments of Bolivia, Peru, and Ecuador broadened their support for quinoa work in the mid-1980s, with Peruvian president Alan García leading the way by propounding an expanded program for traditional Andean agriculture and underutilized Andean crops. Sadly, his program was hampered because prior neglect of the sierra countryside has given the anti-Western Sendero Luminoso (Shining Path) guerrilla movement enough vigor to disrupt government development activities in the highlands, and in all the Andean countries, research and development efforts are cramped by international pressure to pay off debts accumulated by past military governments.

Meanwhile, quinoa is unlikely to establish a solid place in the U.S. market until major food companies start using it in their products. Cooked and cold breakfast cereals, pancake and cornbread mixes, soups and pastas are all likely candidates—but only if processors are assured access to a large-scale supply based on North American production. Nonprofit institutions and risk-taking farmers have made the first moves in that direction, with the former working to select seed, test quinoa under modern cultivation techniques, and find processing machinery, while the latter have applied and modified these findings to suit commercial farming operations. Lacking outside funding, Colorado State University squeezed quinoa research into its ongoing studies of new crops, weed sciences, entomology, and plant physiology even while its research budget was being cut. A number of institutions concerned with alternative agriculture—the Windstar Foundation, the Malachite Small Farm School, the Telluride Institute, the Baca Ranch, and the Talavaya Center—have volunteered sites and labor for research fields, and private farmers have offered additional acreage. Sierra Blanca Associates has raised a small amount of money to support the network, but much more has been given in kind than in funds.

Difficulties have continued to plague research efforts, but by 1987 Colorado State and Sierra Blanca were ready to encourage commercial U.S. production again, and some daring Colorado farmers agreed to take the risk in order to help answer the many questions that could only be answered by experience in large fields. Happily, the results were good, and in October 1987 the first commercial plantings of quinoa outside the Andes were harvested by combine in the fields of Ernie New and several other growers in the San Luis Valley.

At this point, research has succeeded in identifying a seed selection from southern Chile, named "Dave Quinoa" in honor of David Cusack, that has produced consistently well in the short Colorado growing season at sites between 7,000 and 8,500 feet. This variety boasts excellent flavor and nutritional properties and has been found to do well even in the higher latitudes of Canada. Other promising varieties have been identified for elevations in Colorado above 8,500 feet, and Emigdio Ballon, a Bolivian quinoa expert who has worked at the

Talavaya Center since 1985, has selected seed for the warmer New Mexico climate.

Research has progressed on other fronts as well. Fertility tests have confirmed that high yields require the application of substantial quantities of nitrogen. The many kinds of insects that ravaged experimental fields in 1984 have been identified, and work is under way to obtain approval from the Food and Drug Administration for the use of pesticides to combat them. The Pillsbury Company Research Division, cooperating with Meals for Millions to develop a weaning food for babies in Bolivian villages, has tested machinery that efficiently removes saponin from harvested grain.

Even so, by 1989 only three hundred acres were planted in quinoa in Colorado, and yields have been discouraging. Using chemical fertilizers and pesticides would increase the yields, but in the absence of FDA approval for pesticides, all the fields thus far have been organic—and Andean peasants know better how to grow quinoa organically than we do in Colorado. North American production of quinoa has begun to spread, however, and that is a promising development. In 1987, seeds from Colorado and Chile were planted at the 4,000-foot elevation in western Washington State, and in 1988 farmers in Canada began buying seed. Quinoa's low water requirements may make it particularly well suited to the high-elevation wheat belt of western Canada.

On April Fool's Day in 1989 a handful of farmers met at the Sangre de Cristo High School in Mosca, Colorado, to form the North American Quinoa Producers Association, whose name certainly reflects future possibilities more than present actualities. Though the original intent was to create an association confined to Colorado, representatives were on hand from New Mexico, Washington, and Canada, so the new organization, although lacking the funds even to buy stationery, took on the formidable task of encouraging quinoa production and use throughout North America. Concern was voiced at the inaugural meeting that a boom in U.S. quinoa consumption could soon outstrip worldwide production, and while such worry seems premature, major corporations have begun to express interest in quinoa. It seems only a matter of time before one food-processing giant or another, to gain an edge on the competition, will capitalize on quinoa's very positive image by adding it to its products.

In the past five years I have learned to appreciate an early quinoa advocate's remark that "Quinoa has a life of its own." Quinoa seems to use people rather than the other way around. As some have become disheartened, quinoa has attracted new people to take over. Spirits of the Andes may have placed all kinds of obstacles in the path of those trying to preserve and disseminate the "mother grain," but it seems destined nonetheless to take its rightful place among the crops of the world.

Native Crops of the Americas: Passing Novelties or Lasting Contributions to Diversity?

GARY PAUL NABHAN

L̲et us now praise native crops—the fruits, tubers, grains, beans, and greens that have been cultivated in the New World since pre-Columbian times. Some of these food crops have been nurturing cultures in the Americas for the last six to eight millennia. Seeds of these enduring native crop varieties have been passed from hand to hand through as many as one hundred generations of gardeners and farmers since the process of plant domestication began in the New World.

To appraise the genetic changes that have occurred in American plants as a result of this process, botanists seldom have more than a few carbonized seeds, some spikelet chaff, leaf fiber or pollen grains with which to work. Nevertheless, as the preceding chapters make plain, we know with certainty that botanical changes of enormous magnitude have taken place. At the same time, agriculture and concomitant innovations in technology and social organization radically altered the trajectory of many American cultures.

By interpreting a handful of now-famous gourd rinds, minuscule corncobs, and spent bean pods so as to place these materials in their cultural contexts, archaeologists have provided some understanding of the changes that native crop domestication and diffusion have wrought on American civilizations. Yet much of the story remains to be told. Desiccated seeds, coprolite contents, and radiocarbon-dated charcoal must be reconstituted into images of people planting, selecting, harvesting, preparing, and eating their various crops. At the very least, this story includes thousands of pre-Columbian field and orchard crop varieties brought into American households to serve as the *materia prima* for hundreds of distinctive ethnic cuisines.

Perhaps the complexity of crop evolution makes us lose sight of the concurrent cultural evolution of culinary traditions: changes in grinding, roasting, brewing, baking, and curing techniques, not to mention customs of spicing and serving prepared foods. What comes to mind when we imagine pre-Columbian cuisines? Shattering our stereotypes of dreary mushes and charred meats, in *Presencia de la Comida Prehispánica* Teresa Castello Yturbide, Michel Zabe, and Ignacio Pina Lujan elegantly document the preparation of a variety of savory dishes that were first recorded in the early historic codexes and that have persisted to the present in the indigenous communities of Mexico. *Tamales de rana*: Moctezuma's frogs, spiced with *epazote* leaves, *chile pasilla* pods, and chopped prickly pear pads, wrapped together in a corn husk or the skin of an agave leaf and cooked over a hot *comal* made of clay. *Huautli*: the popped seeds of grain amaranth that Dan Early describes, mixed with honey from native bees and sculpted into fantastic forms. *Casuela de iguana*: cleaned and quartered iguana meat stewed in a broth of *jitomate* and *chile costeño* thickened with a ball of maize mush that is mixed into the broth just before serving. *Huazoncle*: flower buds of grain chenopods (like quinoa or lamb's-quarters), stripped off the stalk while still tender, washed in a solution of baking soda, and then cooked in an omelette, perhaps using quail eggs.

To these Mesoamerican recipes we might add *mah-pi*: blue corn balls made by the Missouri River tribes from maize flour moistened with juneberries or blueberries and deer kidney tallow. Or *tarwi con saraphata* from the inter-Andean valley: freshly ground lupine seeds mixed with lime-treated hominy corn, stewed tomatoes, chopped onions, and greens, then boiled to a creamy consistency.

These particular pre-Columbian foods have survived, being prepared today by Native Americans, mestizos, or *ladinos* in much the same manner as they were thousands of years ago. At most, lard or vegetable oils are added, wheat flour is some-times substituted for cornmeal, and a wider range of herbs is used for seasonings. Many, many other indigenous foods, however, are no longer eaten on a routine basis, if at all. Their demise is part of a pattern of profound cultural change that has been correlated with several waves of native crop extir-pation following the arrival of conquistadors, colonists, and diseases from the Old World.

Americans did gain valuable Old World crops through the Columbian Exchange, with remarkable "new foods" such as *mole poblano* arising out of the intermixing of ingredients and hybridization of cooking traditions from the two hemi-spheres, but the Old World crops introduced over the last five centuries have not compensated for the plant diversity lost in the Americas during the same period. The erosion of genetic diversity that began during the half century following Colum-bus has continued almost unabated down to the present. A biological treasure has been squandered; in a very real sense, it has been rendered inaccessible to all of humankind, not just to American cultures.

Since there was no "baseline" inventory of how much variation existed in American fields at the time of Columbus, we will never have a reliable estimate of how much crop diversity—how many genes, vegetable varieties, or plant species—has been lost in the New World during the last five hundred years. (We hardly possess such an inventory for crops that exist today.) Yet fools rush in where archaeobotanists fear to tread. Seed conservationist John Carr hazarded the first guess more than a decade ago, estimating that 70 percent of the crop varieties grown in the Americas prior to Columbus are now extinct. In the U.S. Southwest, my own comparisons of native crop varieties cultivated by prehistoric farmers with those now grown by their descendants suggest that 55 to 65 percent of the region's diversity has been extirpated.

These losses are not just botanical statistics. Vera Bracklin, a Hidatsa Indian whose people's historic fields along the Upper Missouri were inundated by a reservoir, recently gave me her own visceral sense of what has been destroyed: "My grandmother used to raise a lot of beans. On a windy day, she'd put a tarp down. She'd take a panful of uncleaned beans and let the wind blow the leaves away. But then we lost everything. It seems like [our people] lost the Indian way of life when the dam forced their relocation."

To sense how the past five centuries of change have affected crops, diets, and cultures, we must appreciate the way native crop diversity has functioned, the factors that have contributed to its development, and the pressures that have worn part of it away. We must imagine what these crops were as part of the immense fabric of American folklife, woven into a patchwork of fields in rural landscapes.

If you walk through the small, terraced fields tended by Indians in the highlands of central Mexico today, you will see that their cornfields are not monocultural stands of maize. Instead these *milpas* are a collage of greens, beet reds, violets, tans, stripes, and speckles. They are mosaics, with several maize varieties serving as dominant "overstory" crops and many other plants growing up their stalks or in their shadows: grain amaranths, squashes, beans, chili peppers, husk tomatoes or *miltomates, jaltomates*, and semicultivated greens such as *epazote, quintonil*, and *verdolagas*. Domestic turkeys may wander through these heterogeneous patches, picking grasshoppers and tomato hornworms off the plants. The terraced fields are often rimmed with hedges of prickly pear or century plants, and an orchard nearby may feature native capuli cherries and hawthorns along with Spanish-introduced fruits. These food, fiber, and spice crops offer products to be harvested most of the year.

Discussions of American agricultural origins typically emphasize maize—its ancient domestication and primacy in a dietary triumvirate with beans and squash. To be sure, these three crops, each displaying great regional variation, were important in many ways. But American farmers have traditionally relied on a much wider range of crops, and that diversity has had ecological, economic, agronomic, culinary, and nutritional consequences. In summarizing the role that diversity plays in small-scale traditional agriculture, Daniela Soleri and David Cleveland point out, for instance, that different varieties or species of greens may meet largely the same nutritional need but that their physiological and ecological differences increase the reliability of harvests and prolong the period during which greens may be available.

Particularly in unpredictable climates or marginal lands, diversity minimizes the risk of total crop failure, since different crops respond in different ways to droughts, early freezes, insects, and diseases. In heterogeneous fields, some susceptible crops simply escape being seen, smelled, or otherwise located by pests. Faced with a mixture of susceptible and resistant crops maturing at different times, an insect pest is impeded in its evolutionary ability to overcome the resistant gene found in just one of the crop varieties present. Fields that are structurally complex also abound with pest predators, since hedges, vines, upright annuals, and succulents provide nesting and perching sites for birds and other agents of biological control.

Matching specially adapted varieties to field sites with peculiar microclimates, soils, and water sources has the additional virtue of enabling farmers to utilize all the available space for production of one kind or another. Traditional mixed orchard-gardens meet many needs besides those of nutrition. Soleri and Cleveland note: "Some [crops] may provide fruit or vegetables, medicine, building or craft materials, fuel and fodder. Others may be grown for the beauty of their flowers, and all may be grown for market."

Thus, though it is useful to profile single American crops and their culinary uses, it is crucial to keep in mind that each arose in a multidimensional ecological and cultural context. Evolutionary ecologists believe that certain Native American crops truly co-evolved over hundreds of years of native intercropping. Likewise, cultures loosely co-evolved with the sets of plants they domesticated or received from neighboring peoples and adapted for their own uses.

This process of co-evolution began when early farmers started sowing, harvesting, and storing seeds through the winter. These simple actions worked to change the genetic structure of annual plant populations. Teosinte, wild beans, wild gourds, and a few other disturbance-adapted annuals became rapidly, perhaps catastrophically, domesticated. For instance, when beans were harvested and stored in the absence of selection pressures from seed-boring bruchid beetles, previous constraints on seed size, seed coat thickness, and seed coat chemistry were rapidly released. Under subsequent cultural selection, beans became larger and easier to germinate and lost certain bitter chemicals in the seed coat that had once served as feeding deterrents to the beetles.

While Native Americans continued to glean much of their subsistence from wildlands, the initial domestications encouraged many peoples to invest an increasing amount of their effort in tending garden-sized plots of cultivated annuals. These annual crops were not broadcast—not sowed by hand-scattering seeds—in the manner that Old World farmers planted wheat, barley, lentils, and oats, and this fact alone accounts for some of the varietal diversity in New World crops. Native American crops were usually planted in mounds or holes spaced several paces apart. They were probably gathered in a similar fashion—not collectively cut with sickles and then threshed but instead harvested one by one. These practices meant that Native American farmers had great opportunity to notice novel variants. Rather than mass breeding as the Mediterranean wheat sower has done for millennia, the Mesoamerican chili pepper cultivator, the Andean potato farmer, and the arid-American prickly pear propagator became experts at single-plant selection.

Some Mesoamerican *campesinos* continue this tradition today, sorting out each interesting variant, setting its seed aside, and planting that seed in a separate patch the next year to increase its kind. They are connoisseurs of subtle variation and readily take advantage of chance hybrids or somatic mutants that appear in their gardens or field patches. This sort of close cultural selection favors locally specialized ecotypes, farmer-specific flavor and color variants, and culture-specific ceremonial strains of crops.

The number of such folk varieties of crops probably increased dramatically in Mexico during the Late Preclassic and Classic periods around A.D. 100–700, when domesticated annuals became major components of the Mesoamerican diet. As Lawrence and Lucille Kaplan point out, "This was a time of explosive population growth and the founding of new permanent villages and urban centers." A similar shift in agricultural intensification and diversification began a few hundred years later in arid lands that are now part of the U.S. Southwest after communities there became large enough to practice irrigated agriculture along the floodplains of desert rivers. Maize did not become a major dietary component in desert areas until the development of irrigation management by the Hohokam culture.

In South America, crop production in sedentary pottery-making villages began much earlier, perhaps 4,000 to 2,500 years ago. We may assume from studying the fields of their descendants that prehistoric Andean farmers grew more than just a few domesticated crops. They apparently encouraged or at least tolerated a variety of wild greens and semicultivated tubers in their fields, and sporadic outcrossing between wild and cultivated potatoes added to the genetic diversity found in that particular crop. By late prehistoric times there was perhaps a greater varietal diversity within Native American crops than in any era before or since.

Columbus, Cortés, and the conquistadors ushered in the first major decline in New World agricultural diversity. As Alfred Crosby has defined it, the Columbian Exchange included the dispersal to the Americas of dozens of Old World crops, hundreds of weeds, and some major animal pests. With the introduction of livestock, the dispersal of foreign and native plants alike was expedited, their seeds being spread on the hair and muddy hooves and in the feces of cattle, horses, goats, and sheep. Within the first century following Cortés, certain regions of the Americas, such as the Valley of Mexico, were intentionally altered into habitats approximating European pastoral scenes, replete with forage grasses, grain fields, olive orchards, and the like. The inter-Andean valley was also rapidly overhauled, not merely as a visual landscape but also as a food-producing ecosystem.

At the same time, epidemics raged through the Americas, devastating the human population. If ethnohistorian Henry Dobyns's reconstructions are even remotely correct, diseases spread along well-established trade routes in advance of the Spaniards themselves, their effects disrupting both local food production and extra-local exchanges of foodstuffs, medicines, and ceremonial goods. In less than a century, some regions lost three-quarters of their population, leaving in ruins large prehistoric irrigation works once maintained by collective labor. In the southwestern United States, it appears that jack beans, century plants, and grain chenopods were among the crop casualties during this period of turmoil.

As European colonists began to till American soils, Old World crops were planted where native crops once flourished. In a few places, native crops and customs were officially suppressed by the Spanish. During the period between 1690 and 1750, such suppression of native customs led to scattered nativist revivals, some of which temporarily removed the Spanish from positions of power. Whether these nativist movements included traditional crop and food revivals is a topic that invites further attention.

As the Industrial Revolution developed and the population grew in the following centuries, the usurpation of native croplands accelerated. The Europeanization of the American landscape, its farms and crops, has continued well into this century, turning prairies into cereal monocultures, wooded parklands, and pastures as well as converting deserts into artificial (and surely ephemeral) Mediterranean oases. With the advent of farm mechanization and the coalescence of an international market economy, even European-style small farms became disadvantaged. The large industrial farms that took their place certainly did not nurture diversity.

The tragic loss of mixed crops and livestock breeds during the twentieth century has been amply documented in economic and sociological analyses but perhaps never so poignantly conveyed as in *Leaving the Land*, a novel by Douglas Unger. Family farms with a mixture of crops, livestock, and poultry varieties were driven out of business by dovetailing economic and political forces that favored production zones focused on one commodity. As World War II began to affect the American heartland, Unger writes, "lives changed overnight, with crops, livestock, and machinery left in the care of wives, daughters [and older men like Ben Hogan]. . . . The priorities of wartime farming gave Ben Hogan the choice of raising either sugar beets or turkeys." Unger explains the dilemma:

> There was supposed to be a corn shortage for the alcohol industry, alcohol necessary for the manufacture of explosives. But the USDA kept telling farmers that it was simply good sense for a man to raise either sugar beets or turkeys, since both could be processed right away, packed and made ready locally for immediate use. A man was free to raise just corn or wheat or beans, or other livestock animals than turkeys, free to raise many different crops at once in diversified farming, he really

was, there wasn't any law against it. He just wouldn't get much government subsidy money through the Farmers and Ranchers Stabilization Board for those crops, and there were also certain priorities at the Belle Fourche & Western Railroad shipping office. . . . So if a man in Wovoka County wanted to keep raising corn, wheat, beans, beef—diversified crops—just as he always had, he would have to wait several months or more before he could ship his harvest.

Farmers were also put under social and political pressure, told that "The boys overseas need beets and turkeys to win this war." Rural communities suffered further after the war as vertical monopolies forced many families off their land, keeping them from ever farming again. In just a few decades the number of Americans living on farms plummeted from over 50 percent of the nation's population to less than 5 percent.

This trend is mirrored in statistics on Indian farmers in the United States, keepers of the native crops still extant north of Mexico. Between 1887 and 1934, 60 percent of all tribal trust and treaty lands—some eighty-four million acres—passed out of Indian hands as a result of the Dawes Act, a bill designed to promote the assimilation of Indians into the dominant society. Between 1910 and 1982 the number of Indians owning, running, or working on farms in the United States dropped from 48,500 to 7,150 despite an overall increase in the Indian population. As native farmers were forced or lured off the land, centuries-old traditions of planting their families' heirloom seed stocks came to an end.

As if the tragedy at home did not cause enough damage to biodiversity and enough disruption of farming and culinary traditions, the United States began to export its new agricultural scheme to other countries. After World War II, industrial nations led by the United States launched well-intentioned programs to supply hybrid seeds, farm machines, fertilizers, and pesticides to developing nations. As early as 1941, crop geographer Carl Sauer warned policymakers about the impending loss of crop genetic resources and viable cultures, writing, "A good aggressive bunch of American agronomists and plant breeders could ruin the native resources for good by pushing their American commercial stocks. . . . Mexican agriculture cannot be pointed toward standardization on a few commercial types without upsetting native economy and culture hopelessly. The example of Iowa is about the most dangerous of all for Mexico."

Not long ago, I heard these same concerns voiced by an eighty-four-year-old Sonoran farmer who had begun raising food for his family during the Mexican Revolution. "The hybrid corn has no taste," Casimiro Sanchez told me, "and when my neighbors save its seeds to regrow the following year, only small, irregular ears are produced. That's why I save the native seed, but the other people don't anymore. . . . [The community] has lost most of it already."

"Let me predict something," he continued, as we sat in his kitchen, looking at his recent harvest of open-pollinated corn. "If they don't start protecting the native seeds around here, local food production will eventually decline. The quality of the annual crops and even of the fruit trees will fall if we become dependent upon introduced hybrids."

To our permanent disadvantage, the agricultural development foundations undertaking the Green Revolution turned a deaf ear to Sauer's warning and to native concerns, and they failed to study adequately and conserve valuable elements of traditional agro-ecosystems before beginning to change them. Thus their efforts temporarily resulted in higher crop yields per acre in many areas but incurred great biological, environmental, and cultural costs. The question of whether the yield gains were worth more than the losses they caused has been the subject of a long and complex debate.

Finally, another agricultural upheaval is at our door. Called the Gene Revolution, this bag of biotechnological tricks will supposedly enable tropical fruits to be grown in cold-temperate climes by splicing freeze-resistant genes into their germplasm and will turn maize and other nitrogen-consuming cereal crops into nitrogen-fixing plants by stitching into them genes from legumes. Although skepticism about such facile claims is mounting, the combined budget of all the crop genetic engineering firms in North America and Europe has already eclipsed the funds expended by the Green Revolution breeding centers at their peak.

Essential to the development of the biotechnology industry have been legislative and judicial acts enabling private firms to secure proprietary rights to plant genes, previously undescribed species, and novel breeding processes. An individual can now go to a remote farming tribe, collect a previously undescribed crop variety, and take out a patent on it. For example, Palmer's salt grass, once a staple of the Cocopah Indians of the Colorado Delta, has been trademarked as "Wildwheat," and now slightly selected, laboratory-bred cultivars of this ancient food are being patented by a private corporation called Nypa, Inc. Capitalizing on the "Indian heritage" of salt grass cereal, Nypa has marketed it to Nieman Marcus stores as an American gourmet food. Neglecting further study of Palmer's salt grass in its habitat, genetic engineers confidently assert that in a matter of years they will transfer to other cereals this crop's tolerance for salinity. Comparable developments are occurring with blue corn, squashes, chili peppers, and amaranths.

Grave problems lie ahead as these crops pass from the hands

of indigenous farmers to the cryogenic vaults of corporations that see them only as marketable commodities. For example, paddy-grown, fertilized, and pesticide-laden "wild rice" has created stiff economic competition for the Anishinabey, the Ojibway, and other Indian peoples of the Great Lakes region who harvest wild rice by hand and now manage many waterways to conserve this as well as other wild resources. For the Ojibway, the wild rice harvest has been a time for family cooperation, for singing, storytelling, and camping. One Ojibway youth explained to me that the harvest was more than an economic pursuit, that he "just loves the rhythm of the ricing."

As Thomas Vennum has recorded in *Wild Rice and the Ojibway People*, commercial paddy-grown rice is considered a desecration because the first fruits are no longer offered to the Great Spirit; the machine harvesters give the grain a dirty, oily taste; and greed, not sustainability, drives much of the current industry and its product marketing. So adamant are the Ojibway on this point that in 1982, Vennum reports, when a St. Paul food store unwittingly donated paddy-grown rice for a Thanksgiving meal at the American Indian Center, "the Indians refused to take the free rice, even though it meant that their children might go hungry, because the paddy rice offended their cultural and religious sensibilities. Labelling the paddy rice as wild rice was analogous to misrepresenting non-kosher food as kosher."

The Gene Revolution makes fantastic promises to bring exotic foods to our dinner plates, but the ecological and cultural costs that it would entail cannot be easily swept under the dining room rug. It is simply not enough any more to claim that developing new markets for an underexploited crop is a "good" in and of itself. For decades, economic botanists have known of hundreds of good food plants unfamiliar to mainstream agriculture; the challenge before us is to ensure that these worthy old plants are utilized appropriately.

In the climatic zones to which they are adapted, many of the native crops offer commercial farmers lucrative yields with less reliance on irrigation water and chemicals than conventional crops require. That seems appropriate and good, especially when one also factors in other benefits, nutritional and gustatory. Nevertheless, hard questions must be asked, particularly about the appropriation and alteration of crops through the would-be Gene Revolution.

Who benefits? At whose expense? For how long? If blue corn, jicama, or naranjilla are marketed as novelty foods, what lasting benefit will there be? From my point of view, native crops deserve to persist as colorful and nutritious ingredients of truly American cuisines rather than going the way most food fads have gone. They need to become more than the trivial pursuit of gourmet consumers, to provide new benefits for the farmers and gatherers, particularly for those Native Americans who have nurtured and been nurtured by these foodstuffs for centuries.

There *are* appropriate ways to revive these crops, but first we must guarantee their survival. This will take more effort than simply stashing seeds away in gene-bank freezers. Such a technical solution may preserve germplasm, but it does not conserve the dynamic cultural context of the seed stocks, nor does it allow for their continued evolution and adaptation to changing conditions.

Dozens of groups, mostly small and community-based, are now involved in the search for alternative, culturally supportive means of perpetuating genetic diversity in American crops. The endeavor I am closest to, Native Seeds/SEARCH, is centered in Tucson and in the last decade has collected and redistributed seeds to more than two dozen tribes in the U.S.

Southwest and northwestern Mexico. Hundreds of folk varieties of fifteen pre-Columbian crops are kept in the gene bank at Native Seeds/SEARCH, but its primary goal is to see them conserved and utilized in the gardens and fields of the region to which they belong, to which they are adapted. Often, Indian farmers have asked for help in relocating a variety they have inadvertently lost, and the Native Seeds/SEARCH staff, encountering that particular variety in a more remote village, has been able to return it to them. In several cases that we know of, once reintroduced, these seed stocks have been grown again, season after season, up to the present time.

In other cases, it takes more than a simple reintroduction to allow native crop diversity to continue; action must also be taken to reduce the pressures working against diversity. For several decades, applied anthropologists have helped rural development projects to direct Indian cultures *away* from their traditional ways of small-scale farming. Now it is time for the anthropology of resistance to be practiced in the service of native peoples who wish to retain or restore their agricultural heritage in the face of outside pressures to abandon it.

Two exemplary groups, Cultural Survival and the Seventh Generation Fund, are active in assisting native communities to maintain their land-based way of life. By providing legal, social, and development services guided by the communities themselves, these organizations have offered timely assistance in thwarting deleterious development plans and have encouraged the emergence of leadership skills within the communities so that such aid will be unnecessary in the future.

Once such communities are relatively secure from immediate external threats and their basic set of indigenous resources is conserved, they may find several appropriate ways to revive their native crops. For example, participants in the Navajo Family Farms Project, based near Leupp, Arizona, are raising blue corn for consumption first at local schools and elderly programs, planning to sell only their surplus corn off the reservation. Similarly, the Ikwe Marketing Collective of the Anishinabey Indians in Minnesota encourages its members to reserve as much of their hand-harvested wild rice as they want for themselves before selling their harvest to health-food stores. As Winona LaDuke explains, "By consuming our resources, we get a 'use value.' This value—whether from eating wild-rice or berries—is critical to our poor community. . . . To feed our families, we might as well eat good native food instead of trying to get the money to buy 'White' food."

The persistence of agricultural and culinary traditions is of paramount concern to many of the Native American people. It may not be possible to "reconstruct" the original context of native foods, nor would many Native Americans necessarily want to revive bygone diets. Nostalgia is not the driving sentiment in this movement, as some critics would have it. Instead, it is powered by a sincere and sensible interest in retaining and renovating aspects of the native agricultural and culinary traditions in order to preserve nutritional, aesthetic, cultural, and ecological values embedded in them.

For the rest of us, it also makes good sense to support a revival of traditional agriculture in the Americas. To gain access to traditional foods is an appealing reason but hardly the only one. Even if we ourselves are not growing or eating many of the ancient American crop varieties, they currently serve—and will continue to serve—as the primary resources for plant breeding programs seeking to increase the resistance of commercial crops to insects, disease, drought, and frost.

Globally, farmers face a changing climate, diminishing supplies of irrigation water and cheap chemical fertilizers, and the perennial problem of virulent new strains of pathogens. Old grain and bean varieties grown by native farmers are the backup force required to stave off famine should calamity strike the fields where major varieties are grown in monocultures over thousands of contiguous acres. Without the reservoir of traditional varieties to draw upon, an epidemic, plague, or climatic shift might abruptly turn the breadbasket regions of the world into basket cases. For any future stability in the global food supply, diversity must be restored to all major food crops.

We also need to reform agricultural practices, and here, too, native farming has much to teach us. As noted earlier, Native American farmers have typically intercropped several cultivated species in each field as a means of producing more food, forage, or fiber from a single piece of ground. Such polycultures—crops mixed in the same field—create greater habitat heterogeneity for field-dwelling animals and reduce the probability of a population explosion by any single pest. The majority of indigenous farmers still practice intercropping, and non-Indians are now learning how heterogeneous agricultural "communities" can be managed with little or no petrochemicals, high-tech pest control, or intensive irrigation and cultivation. Even the so-called "new ideas" of alternative agriculture—Bill Mollison's permaculture and Wes Jackson's herbaceous perennial polycultures of prairie natives—build on intercropping concepts long practiced by indigenous farmers.

It is clear that both the crop genes and traditional knowledge still husbanded by Native American farmers have value to modern-day mainstream agriculture and will continue to have value in the future. This genetic and folk-scientific information cannot simply be expropriated without causing certain losses; it is most complete and valuable when conserved in place. However stress-tolerant the plants may be in the field, however nutritious they may be in any diet, they evolved to fit particular cultural and environmental contexts. Their beauty is derived from this fitness.

To praise appropriately the bean vines twining up stalks of maize or heirloom chili peppers outcrossing with wild chiltepines in nearby hedgerows, we must also praise the cultures that first observed them, then tolerated or intentionally nurtured them. Ultimately, the most potent way of conserving biological diversity may be to protect the diversity of the cultures that have stewarded the plant and animal communities upon which our agriculture is based.

Food Plants of American Origin

What follows is only a partial list of food plants indigenous to the Americas. Where a common name carries an asterisk, not all of the plants known by that name are of American origin.

COMMON NAME	SCIENTIFIC NAME
achira, Queensland arrowroot	*Canna edulis*
agave, century plant	*Agave* species
ahipa	*Pachyrrhizus ahipa*
alligator pear. *See* avocado	
allspice	*Pimenta diocia*
amaranth, huautli, kiwicha	*Amaranthus* species
arracacha	*Arracacia xanthorrhiza*
avocado, alligator pear	*Persea americana*
beans:	
common bean	*Phaseolus vulgaris*
lima bean, sieva bean	*Phaseolus lunatus*
scarlet runner bean	*Phaseolus coccineus*
tepary bean	*Phaseolus acutifolius*
Bell pepper. *See* chili pepper	

blackberry	*Rubus* species
black raspberry	*Rubus* species
black walnut. *See* walnut	
blueberry	*Vaccinium corymbosum*
Brazil nut	*Bertholletia excelsa*
cacao (chocolate, cocoa)	*Theobroma cacao*
cainito, star apple	*Chrysophyllum cainito*
Cape gooseberry, poha, goldenberry	*Physalis peruviana*
capuli cherry	*Prunus capuli*
cashew	*Anacardium occidentale*
cassava. *See* manioc	
century plant. *See* agave	
chayote	*Sechium edule*
cherimoya	*Annona cherimola*
chia	*Salvia hispanica*
chico. *See* sapote (yellow)	
chili pepper	*Capsicum* species
chocolate. *See* cacao	
chokecherry	*Prunus virginiana*
cocoa. *See* cacao	
cocoña, topiru	*Solanum sessiliflorum*
corn. *See* maize	
cranberry	*Vaccinium macrocarpon*
cupuaçu	*Theobroma grandiflorum*
currants*	*Ribes* species
custard apple	*Annona reticulata*
epazote, Mexican tea	*Chenopodium ambrosiodes*
goldenberry. *See* Cape gooseberry	
gooseberry	*Ribes* species
granadilla. *See* passion fruit	
grapes*	*Vitus* species
guava	*Psidium guajava*
hawthorn*	*Crataegus coccinea*
hickory nut	*Carya ovata*
hog plum	*Spondias* species

huautli. *See* amaranth
husk tomato. *See* tomatillo
ice-cream bean. *See* pacay
jack bean   *Canavalia ensiformis*
jaltomate   *Jaltomata procumbens*
Jerusalem artichoke, sunchoke   *Helianthus tuberosus*
jicama   *Pachyrrhizus erosus*
jitomate. *See* tomato
jojoba (edible seeds, oil)   *Simmondsia chinensis*
kaniwa   *Chenopodium pallidicaule*
kiwicha. *See* amaranth
lulo. *See* naranjilla
maca   *Lepidium meyenii*
maize, corn   *Zea mays*
miltomate. *See* tomatillo
mamey. *See* sapote (yellow)
mammee apple   *Mammea americana*
manioc, cassava   *Manihot esculenta*
mashua   *Tropaeolum tuberosum*
mauka   *Mirabilis expansa*
Mexican oregano   *Lippia* species
Mexican tea. *See* epazote
miltomate. *See* tomatillo
naranjilla, lulo   *Solanum quitoense*
oca   *Oxalis tuberosa*
pacay, ice-cream bean   *Inga* species
Palmer's salt grass   *Distichlis palmeri*
palm heart   *Euterpe* species
panic grass   *Panicum sonorum*
papaya, pawpaw   *Carica* species,
          esp. *C. papaya*
passion fruit, granadilla   *Passiflora* species
pawpaw. *See* papaya
peach palm   *Bactris gasipaes*
peanut   *Arachis hypogaea*

pecan	*Carya illinoinesis*
pepino	*Solanum muricatum*
pepper. *See* chili pepper	
persimmon*	*Diospyrus virginiana*
pineapple	*Ananas comosus*
piñon pine nut	*Pinus edulis*
pinuelo	*Bromelia* species
poha. *See* Cape gooseberry	
potato	*Solanum tuberosum*
prickly pear	*Opuntia* species
pumpkin	*Cucurbita pepo*
Queensland arrowroot. *See* Achira	
quinoa	*Chenopodium quinoa*
quintonil	*Amaranthus retroflexus*
quito palm	*Parajubaea cocoides*
raspberry	*Rubus idaeus* var. *strigosus*
sapote (black)	*Diospyros digyna*
sapote (white)	*Casimiroa edulis*
sapote (yellow), mamey	*Pouteria mammosa*
soursop	*Annona muricata*
squash,* including:	
crookneck squash	*Cucurbita moschata*
cushaw	*Cucurbita argyrosperma*
winter squash (including acorn and hubbard)	*Cucurbita maxima*
zucchini	*Cucurbita pepo*
star apple. *See* cainito	
strawberry	*Fragaria x Ananassa*
sugar maple	*Acer saccharum*
sunchoke. *See* Jerusalem artichoke	
sunflower	*Helianthus annuus*
Surinam cherry	*Eugenia uniflora*
sweet potato	*Ipomoea batatas*
tamarillo, tree tomato	*Cyphomandra betacea*
tarwi	*Lupinus mutabilis*

tomatillo, husk tomato, miltomate	*Physalis ixocarpa*
tomato	*Lycopersicon esculentum*
topiru. *See* cocoña	
tree tomato. *See* tamarillo	
ulluco	*Ullucos tuberosus*
vanilla	*Vanilla planifolia*
verdolagas	*Portulaca oleracea*
walnuts	*Juglans* species
wild rice	*Zizania aquatica*
yacon	*Polymnia sonchifolia*

Recommendations for Further Reading

OF GENERAL INTEREST

Anderson, Edgar. *Plants, Man and Life*. Berkeley: University of California Press, 1969.

Berry, Wendell. *The Gift of Good Land: Further Essays Cultural and Agricultural*. San Francisco: North Point Press, 1981.

——— . "The Pleasures of Eating." In *Our Sustainable Table*, Robert Clark, ed. San Francisco: North Point Press, 1990.

Clark, Robert, ed. *Our Sustainable Table*. San Francisco: North Point Press, 1990.

Crosby, Alfred W., Jr. *The Columbian Exchange: Biological and Cultural Consequences of 1492*. Westport, Conn.: Greenwood Press, 1972.

——— . *Ecological Imperialism: The Biological Expansion of Europe, 900–1900*. Cambridge: Cambridge University Press, 1986.

Fowler, Cary, and Pat Mooney. *Shattering: Food, Politics, and the Loss of Genetic Diversity*. Tucson: University of Arizona Press, 1990.

Heiser, Charles B. *Of Plants and People*. Norman: University of Oklahoma Press, 1985.

Hyams, Edward. *Plants in the Service of Man: 10,000 Years of Domestication*. Philadelphia: J. B. Lippincott Company, 1971.

Jackson, Wes, Wendell Berry, and Bruce Coleman, eds. *Meeting the Expectations of the Land: Essays in Sustainable Agriculture and Stewardship*. San Francisco: North Point Press, 1984.

McGee, Harold. *On Food and Cooking: The Science and Lore of the Kitchen*. New York: Charles Scribner's Sons, 1984.

Nabhan, Gary Paul. *Enduring Seeds: Native American Agriculture and Wild Plant Conservation*. San Francisco: North Point Press, 1989.

Sauer, Carl O. *Agricultural Origins and Dispersals*. New York: American Geographical Society, 1952.

Sokolov, Raymond. *Why We Eat What We Eat*. New York: Summit Books, 1991.

Viola, Herman J., and Carolyn Margolis, eds. *Seeds of Change: A Quincentennial Commemoration*. Washington, D.C.: Smithsonian Institution Press, 1991.

CHAPTER 1. ENCOUNTERS WITH NEW WORLD FOODS

Crosby, Alfred W., Jr. *The Columbian Exchange: Biological and Cultural Consequences of 1492*. Westport, Conn.: Greenwood Press, 1972.

Davidson, Alan, ed. *Food in Motion: Proceedings of the Oxford Symposium on Food History*. London: Prospect Books, 1983.

Grewe, Rudolf. "The Arrival of the Tomato in Spain and Italy: Early Recipes." In *Journal of Gastronomy* 3 (Summer 1987).

Salaman, Redcliffe N. *The History and Social Influence of the Potato*. 3d ed. J. G. Hawkes, ed. Cambridge: Cambridge University Press, 1985.

CHAPTER 2. THE RENAISSANCE OF AMARANTH

Cole, John. *Amaranth: From the Past for the Future*. Emmaus, Pa.: Rodale Press, 1979.

Early, Daniel K. "Amaranth Secrets of the Aztecs." In *Organic Gardening* (December 1977): 69–73.

Heiser, Charles. *Of Plants and People*. Norman: University of Oklahoma Press, 1985.

Nabhan, Gary Paul. *Gathering the Desert*. Tucson: University of Arizona Press, 1987.

National Research Council. *Lost Crops of the Incas: Little-Known Plants of the Andes with Promise for Worldwide Cultivation*. Washington, D.C.: National Academy Press, 1989.

———. *Amaranth: Modern Prospects for an Ancient Crop*. Washington, D.C.: National Academy Press, 1983.

Safford, William E. "A Forgotten Cereal of Ancient America." In *Proceedings of the 19th International Congress of Americanists*. Washington, D.C., 1915.

CHAPTER 3. VANILLA

Childers, Norman F., Hector R. Cibes, and Ernesto Hernandez-Medina, "Vanilla: The Orchid of Commerce." In *The Orchids: A Scientific Survey*, Carl L. Withner, ed. New York: Ronald Press Co., 1959.

Rain, Patricia. *Vanilla Cookbook*. Berkeley, Calif.: Celestial Arts, 1986.

Root, Waverly. *Food*. New York: Simon and Schuster, 1980.

CHAPTER 4. MAIZE

Beadle, George. "The Mystery of Maize." Chicago: Field Museum of Natural History, 1972.

Galinat, Walton C. "The Domestication and Diffusion of Maize." In *Prehistoric Food Production in North America*, Richard I. Ford, ed. Anthropological Papers, no. 75. Ann Arbor: University of Michigan Press, 1985.

———. "The Evolution of Corn." In *Advances in Agronomy*, Donald L. Sparks, ed. San Diego: Academic Press, forthcoming.

Weatherwax, Paul. *Indian Corn in Old America*. New York: Macmillan Publishing Co., 1954.

CHAPTER 5. BEANS OF THE AMERICAS

Duke, James A. *Handbook of Legumes of World Economic Importance.* New York: Plenum Press, 1981.

Gepts, Paul, ed. *Genetic Resources of* Phaseolus *Beans.* Dordrecht, Netherlands: Kluwer Academic Publishers, 1988.

Kaplan, Lawrence. "New World Beans." In *Horticulture* (October 1980): 43–49.

National Research Council. *Tropical Legumes: Resources for the Future.* Washington, D.C.: National Academy Press, 1975.

CHAPTER 6. CHILI PEPPERS

Andrews, Jean. *Peppers: The Domesticated Capsicums.* Austin: University of Texas Press, 1984.

Eshbaugh, W. H., S. I. Guttman, and M. J. McLeod. "The Origin and Evolution of Domesticated Capsicum Species." In *Journal of Ethnobiology* 3 (1): 49–54.

Halasz, Zoltan. *Hungarian Paprika Through the Ages.* Budapest: Corvina Press, 1963.

Heiser, Charles B. *Of Plants and People.* Norman: University of Oklahoma Press, 1985.

Pickersgill, Barbara. "Migrations of Chili Peppers, *Capsicum* Species, in the Americas." In *Pre-Columbian Plant Migration*, Doris Stone, ed. Cambridge, Mass.: Harvard University Press, 1984.

CHAPTER 7. ANDEAN ROOT CROPS

National Research Council. *Lost Crops of the Incas: Little-Known Plants of the Andes with Promise for Worldwide Cultivation.* Washington, D.C.: National Academy Press, 1989.

CHAPTER 8. CACAO AND CHOCOLATE

Cook, L. R., and E. H. Meursing. *Chocolate Production and Use.* New York: Harcourt Brace Jovanovich, 1982.

Huntford, Roland. *Scott and Amundsen: The Race to the South Pole.* New York: Atheneum, 1984.

Minifie, B. W. *Chocolate, Cocoa and Confectionary: Science and Technology*, 3d ed. New York: Van Nostrand Reinhold, 1989.

Morton, Marcia, and Frederic Morton. *Chocolate: An Illustrated History*. New York: Crown, 1986.

Wagner, Gillian. *The Chocolate Conscience*. London: Chatto and Windus, 1988.

Wood, G.A.R., and R. A. Lass. *Cocoa*. 4th ed. New York: Macmillan Publishing Co., 1985.

CHAPTER 9. QUINOA

Eiselen, Elizabeth. "Quinoa, a Potentially Important Food Crop of the Andes." *Journal of Geography* 55 (October 1956): 330–333.

National Research Council. *Lost Crops of the Incas: Little-Known Plants of the Andes with Promise for Worldwide Cultivation*. Washington, D.C.: National Academy Press, 1989.

Risi, J. C., and N. W. Galwey. "The *Chenopodium* Grains of the Andes: Inca Crops for Modern Agriculture." *Advanced Applied Biology* 10 (1984): 145–216.

Wood, Rebecca. *Quinoa the Supergrain: Ancient Food for Today*. New York: Japan Publications, 1989.

EPILOGUE

Castello Yturbide, Teresa; Michel Zabe; and Ignacio Pina Lujan. *Presencia de la Comida Prehispánica*. Mexico City: Fomento Cultural Banamex, 1987.

Crosby, Alfred W., Jr. *The Columbian Exchange: Biological and Cultural Consequences of 1492*. Westport, Conn.: Greenwood Press, 1972.

——— . *Ecological Imperialism: The Biological Expansion of Europe 900–1900*. Cambridge: Cambridge University Press, 1986.

Kaplan, Lawrence, and Lucille N. Kaplan. "*Phaseolus* in Archaeology." In *Genetic Resources of Phaseolus Beans*, Paul Gepts, ed. Dordrecht, Netherlands: Kluwer Academic Publishers, 1988.

Sauer, Carl O. Quoted in Angus Wright, "Innocents Abroad: American Agricultural Research in Mexico." In *Meeting the Expectations of the Land: Essays in Sustainable Agriculture and Stewardship*, Wes Jackson, Wendell Berry, and Bruce Coleman, eds. San Francisco: North Point Press, 1984.

Soleri, Daniela, and David A. Cleveland. "Diversity and Small-Scale Traditional Agriculture." *Seedhead News* [Native Seeds/SEARCH, Tucson, Ariz.] 23:6–7.

Unger, Douglas. *Leaving the Land*. New York: Harper and Row, 1984.

Vennum, Thomas, Jr. *Wild Rice and the Ojibway People*. St. Paul: Minnesota Historical Society, 1988.

Notes on the Contributors

JEAN ANDREWS, a naturalist, artist, writer, and gourmet chef, is the author of *Peppers: the Domesticated Capsicums*, the definitive work on chili peppers. Dr. Andrews is at work on a second book on capsicums that will focus on their use in cooking.

LINDA CORDELL is the Irvine Curator at the California Academy of Sciences and chairs its Department of Anthropology. A specialist in native cultures of the southwestern United States, Dr. Cordell has directed extensive archaeological fieldwork in that area and has published, among other works, a *Prehistory of the Southwest*.

ALAN DAVIDSON is a British historian, former diplomat, author, and co-founder and director of Prospect Books. He has lectured and written extensively on food history and is preparing the *Oxford Companion to Food* for publication by the Oxford University Press.

DANIEL EARLY, an anthropologist whose research and publications focus on Native American agriculture and food technology, has played a leading role in field studies of modern amaranth cultivation. Dr. Early teaches at Central Oregon Community College in Bend.

NELSON FOSTER, a writer and editor, concentrates on topics of natural history, native traditions, social issues, and religion. His particular interest, and the focus of his writing and editorial work, is Hawaii and other islands of the Pacific.

WALTON GALINAT has made a lifelong study of the origin and evolution of maize and is a world authority on the subject. Recently retired from a professorship at the University of Massachusetts, he continues to conduct research on maize and to add to the list of more than 350 publications that bear his name.

LAWRENCE KAPLAN is a professor of biology at the University of Massachusetts in Boston. An ethnobotanist, he specializes in the origin and evolution of the *Phaseolus* beans and the analysis of archaeological plant remains, and he has published widely on these topics in both the scholarly and the popular press.

LUCILLE N. KAPLAN, an anthropologist, has frequently collaborated with her husband, Lawrence Kaplan, in studying and publishing on topics of pre-Columbian bean agriculture and use. A lecturer at the University of Massachusetts in Boston, she teaches courses on Mesoamerica and peasant societies.

JOHN MCCAMANT heads Sierra Blanca Associates, the nonprofit organization that introduced quinoa in the United States. Dr. McCamant is a professor at the Graduate School of International Studies at the University of Denver and has been an organic gardener for forty-five years.

GARY NABHAN, an ethnobotanist, writer, and co-founder of Native Seeds/SEARCH, devotes himself to the preservation of traditional plants and lifeways of the Sonoran Desert region. Dr. Nabhan's books include *The Desert Smells Like Rain*, *Gathering the Desert*, and *Enduring Seeds: Native American Agriculture and Wild Plant Conservation*.

PATRICIA RAIN is a writer and communications consultant with a background in anthropology. Much of her work focuses on food and health subjects, and she is the author of three cookbooks, including *The Vanilla Cookbook*.

NOEL VIETMEYER is a leading student and apostle of little-known plants, animals, and technologies of the Americas. Author and editor of important technical and popular publications in this field, Dr. Vietmeyer works at the National Research Council in Washington, D.C.

JOHN WEST, professor of botany at the University of California at Berkeley, focuses his research on the biosystematics of marine algae and the agriculture and technology of cacao. He is the author of many scholarly articles on these topics and advises cacao producers in Latin America and the Pacific basin.

Index